Also by Bill Good

Prospecting Your Way to Sales Success

HOT
PROSPECTS

THE PROVEN PROSPECTING SYSTEM
TO RAMP UP YOUR SALES CAREER

Bill Good

SCRIBNER

New York   London   Toronto   Sydney

SCRIBNER
A Division of Simon & Schuster, Inc.
1230 Avenue of the Americas
New York, NY 10020

This Scribner hardcover edition August 2008

SCRIBNER and design are trademarks of The Gale Group, Inc.,
used under license by Simon & Schuster, Inc., the publisher of this work.

For information about special discounts for bulk purchases,
please contact Simon & Schuster Special Sales at
1-800-456-6798 or business@simonandschuster.com.

DESIGNED BY ERICH HOBBING

Text set in Sabon

Manufactured in the United States of America

10   9   8   7   6   5   4   3   2   1

Library of Congress Cataloging-in-Publication Data available

ISBN-13: 978-1-4516-4826-3

Portions of this work were previously published in
Prospecting Your Way to Sales Success by Scribner.

A sign in countless sales offices reads:
"Until someone sells something, nothing happens."

This book is dedicated to the millions of salespeople
who make something happen and on whom our economy
and prosperity depend.

Acknowledgments

Thank You Very Much

For working so hard to make this book a reality:

Roz Lippel, associate publisher of Scribner and my editor. Your patient nudging, encouragement, and suggestions helped more than you know.

Kara Watson, Scribner publishing manager. You helped me take this project from manuscript to finished book.

Bill Drennan, copyeditor. You make me look good . . . er . . . well?

Jenny Good, my daughter, a wonderful "touch the heart" writer, for your tireless proofing, suggestions, and help on the manuscript.

My staff at Bill Good Marketing for giving me the time to write the book. To name only two, Jill Olsen, president, there from the beginning, and Michelle Cummings, senior vice president–Operations, who came through at the last minute with a much needed fresh pair of eyes, rooting out a final nest of errors.

For helping make my life worthwhile:

Joava. When first I saw a pretty girl in a long white dress, I thought, "She's for me." It's never changed. Thank you for believing, sometimes when I didn't.

Bret Good, our only son. I am so glad you knocked on our door many moons ago. You became part of our lives and then officially part of our family. And then you met and married our beautiful Lori. How lucky we are.

ACKNOWLEDGMENTS

Nicci Good Stokes and her husband, Devin. For being great parents, raising beautiful smart kids. Justin, Chloe, and Lucas, I love you all very much. I'm so proud of the good example you all set.

Again Jenny, now Jenny Good Widmaier, always my dollop of sunshine. And Frantz, thank you for coming into our lives. Together, you and Jenny brought us Maximus, our newest grandson.

Contents

CONTENTS

BOOK THREE

Lead Development

179

HOT
PROSPECTS

BOOK ONE

The Good Way
to Prospect

A Working Book

This is a book for salespeople, sales managers, and business owners who want to improve their sales results in today's changed sales environment.

Make no mistake: we are in a new sales era. This era officially began in July 2003, when the "Do Not Call" Registry was implemented by the Federal Trade Commission.* While it is still possible to call people at home, when tens of millions of people flocked to sign up, they told sales professionals and their management teams in no uncertain terms: Do Not Call Me at Home! If you listen carefully, they really don't want you calling them *unsolicited* at work, either.

Part of my intent with this book is to help you work through these challenges and achieve sales success despite the anticontact movement currently under way.

This is not a motivational book. I don't have parables about mice moving cheese. These fables might make you feel good for a few hours or days, and there is a time and a place for these, but not here. If you want one of the "feel good" books, log on to Amazon, search for "Motivational," and you'll find more than fifty-five thousand choices.

This is a working book.

You don't improve your skill just by reading about techniques and ideas. You improve it by working at it; hence the idea that this is a working book.

Now, let's get to work.

This is really more than a book. On the website at www.hot prospectsbook.com, you will find supplemental documents and resources to help you build your business to the next level.

* http://www.ftc.gov/opa/2003/03/donotcall.shtm.

How about:

31 letters
24 scripts
 6 checklists
 1 white paper* template
 3 letter templates
 4 sample direct-mail letters
 1 web resources page
 1 sales profile
 2 bonus chapters

To gain access to the website, follow the registration procedure at www.hotprospectsbook.com.

Once you register and fill out your data sheet, the letters you download will be customized with all of your information: your name, your company, your phone number, your address. Save them to your hard drive, and you can go to work, undoubtedly with a little editing on your part. The same goes for the scripts. Instead of "This is FNAME LNAME with COMPANY NAME," it will say, "This is Barb Barking with the Acme Company here in Cleveland."

Use the letter templates to help you develop powerful letters, faxes, and emails.

The web resources page will direct you to our current recommended web pages, which will help you get your job done better and faster.

The sales profile is a complete set of documents to help you build your own extremely powerful sales profile.

I have buried passwords throughout the pages of this book. Each chapter has its own password to access the chapter-specific content on the website. There is also a master password that gives you access to the site itself. When you register on the website for the first time, you will be able to create the master password.

The passwords in this book are not boldfaced, boxed, or otherwise set off. They are just part of the text. You have to read the book to find them.

See what I mean about this being a working book?

You're working already.

---

* A white paper is a short document used to help educate customers about the product or service they will be purchasing or investing in. It is called a white paper because the document itself was initially bound in white paper.

1

Hot Prospects

A Millionaire Sales Strategy

Suppose your goal is to become a millionaire—an objective already achieved by countless small-business owners and savvy sales professionals.

According to Tom Stanley, a millionaire himself and author of *The Millionaire Next Door,* 32 percent of millionaires are business owners; 16 percent are corporate executives; 10 percent are attorneys; and 9 percent are physicians. The rest are accountants, sales professionals, engineers, professors, etc. Stanley notes, "A disproportionately high percentage of millionaires, multimillionaires, and decamillionaires are self employed business owners and entrepreneurs or self employed professionals."

Since others have done it, why not you? (If this is not your goal, gently slide this book back on the shelf and order a copy of *Your Retirement: Scraping By on Social Security.*)

Okay. You're still with me. You are not buying *Scraping By.* . . .

Obviously, the reason you struck out on your own as a business owner or sales professional is that you want a measure of success beyond what you can achieve as an office worker. While you may not have current plans to retire immediately, and hopefully you enjoy what you do, sooner or later you will either hang it up or slow it down. Wouldn't it be nice to have the freedom to choose how and where you will live and be able to maintain the lifestyle to which you've now grown accustomed?

To accomplish this goal, you must implement three broad strategies:

1. Make more money (which means make more sales).
2. Control spending.
3. Invest your surplus wisely and systematically.

Make it. Save it. Grow it.

This book is about making it.

If you are in sales, this book is for you.

If you manage salespeople, this book is for you.

If you own a business that employs salespeople, once again, this book is for you.

I will focus mainly on sales success in this book. But first I want to say a word about saving money and growing it.

In his book *The Automatic Millionaire,* David Bach—a client of mine before he became the bestselling author of *Smart Women Finish Rich*—created a plan almost anyone can use to create a seven-figure net worth. I suggest you read *The Automatic Millionaire* and consider it as a companion volume to this book. What's the point of making it if you don't invest and grow it correctly?

Reading *The Automatic Millionaire,* you will discover two related factors working against you: time and the amount you invest.

If you start early, create the surplus, and then systematically invest, you will make it. But start late—as many readers are painfully aware—and it's tougher, a *lot* tougher. You have to make *and invest* a lot more. Otherwise, *Scraping By on Social Security* will be your companion volume in the last third of your life.

If you are a late bloomer, you need to *make a lot more money* so you can save and invest it. You should probably start with David Bach's *Start Late/Finish Rich*.

START WITH A DOUBLE

My goal for this book is help you double your business.

Pie in the sky?

Hardly. In the past twenty years, the professional staff at my company, Bill Good Marketing, and I have coached countless salespeople to and beyond—way beyond—a double. Some liked the "double" goal so much that they repeated it a third time and some even a fourth. The success we have enjoyed has allowed us to confidently position ourselves as "number one in sales and marketing systems in the financial services industry." If you question what I just said, and if you have a financial planner or broker, just ask him or her, "Do you know Bill Good?" The answer will be "Yes." While we have achieved that top position in financial services, the sales market in countless other industries is not all that different. My more than twenty-five years of knowledge and experience in financial services are applicable to any sales professional or business owner who has a decent size market, sells a relatively high-priced product or service, and needs more clients and prospects.

The ideas in this book are the foundation for a product we have sold since 1986. I immodestly named it the Bill Good Marketing System. We position it as a computer-based, client-marketing, prospecting, and office-management system. I designed it for companies whose product is relatively expensive and therefore must be sold. It would not be appropriate for a dry cleaner or a hardware store. The primary products or services must be sold as opposed to bought (as through a retail store).

Its mission: to enable our clients to create the time and money to pursue other goals in life.

Reflect for a moment on what you want to accomplish. Whatever you desire requires time and probably money. Time and money sit on opposite ends of an energy spectrum. To accomplish your important goals, you might need more time. You might need more money. Most likely you need some of both.

Our system and the ideas in this book are dedicated to helping you double your income or work half as much with the obvious understanding that there are countless waypoints between these two goals.

The mission is ours; the goal is yours.

YOU ARE NOT A FINANCIAL ADVISER; DOES THIS APPLY TO YOU?

Challenges with marketing, prospecting, selling, and organizing are common to most companies.

While I am not and never will be a financial adviser or planner, I learned most of my craft in that industry. Whether you are in financial services, commercial real estate, or run the sales and catering division of a hotel, the skills are all essentially the same.

Although Bill Good Marketing is not a financial planning firm, internally we use the same tools we teach financial planners, and these are the same tools you need.

Same skills, different market.

Although many of the examples I use are from financial services, don't even think for a second that these examples may not fit you perfectly.

While I've worked mostly in the financial services industry, the methods I use have been applied to people as far from financial services as you can get. We have had stunning success stories from people in software sales, real estate, auto sales, and even a stay-at-home mom who was able to employ some of the same techniques from my first book and get her income to the point where she could stay at home *and* live well.

Years of experience have taught me that if you implement the strategies outlined in this book, you can double your income in two to three years. If you keep spending under control and invest systematically, time will be on your side.

So if having a great career, building a wonderful business, and retiring well-off are what you see for yourself, you have come to the right place to learn "The Good Way."

THE FORK IN THE ROAD

What is our strategy to help you increase your sales and income?

Yogi Berra once said, "When you come to a fork in the road, take it."

You are there now, at the proverbial fork in the road.

One fork we could take leads to the hilltop, a fortified castle called "power selling." Take that route, eat bowls of rusty nails each morning, and each day ride out and *close the sale.*

The other fork takes you to a township of "hot prospects."

This route focuses on getting you in front of more hot prospects. I will give you an exact definition of this term later, but you know hot prospects. You live for them. With hot prospects, you don't really need all that "power selling, champion closing, dynamic" blah blah blah preached so passionately by countless sales trainers.

Perhaps there is a time and a place for power selling. But in this book we will be taking the other fork in the road, toward the township of hot prospects.

THE ROUTE TO POWER SELLING

In my sarcastic rejection of the trip to power selling, I exaggerated a bit. Now let's tell the truth.

Selling skills—the ability to create desire to have the benefits of your product—and closing skills—the ability to get people to make a decision about buying your product—are vital to success as a sales professional.

From my experience, a "newbie" salesperson learns to sell quickly (or doesn't get it at all). Within the first couple of years, he or she must learn presentation skills, how to handle objections, and how to close.

By failing to master these vital skills, the new salesperson takes a sharp detour off the road to sales success and winds up thrashing around in the jungle of employment opportunities elsewhere. Sometimes one takes this cutoff voluntarily, but oftentimes not.

Without selling skills, there is no sales career. However, once the newbie gets it, and the selling skills improve, the increase in commissions will only be incremental. You won't get a two-to-three-year double just because you have merely improved your selling skills. And we're not interested in incremental improvements.

We're interested in quantum leaps.

The first jump comes from mastering the skills that will help you create more and better prospects.

I will assume that your selling skills, while always capable of improvement, are adequate enough that you can persuade a decent percent of the people you talk with to buy your product.

The goal, however, is more hot prospects.

This translates to closing more and bigger sales, and doing it faster.

More. Bigger. Faster. That's our mission.

2

The Old Way vs. the Good Way

The lack of money is the root of all evil.
—Bill Good, age nine

Until this very moment, you were not aware that I, Bill Good, am the creator of many of the world's most famous statements. In some cases, just for fun, such as the above statement, I took an earlier famous statement of mine and reversed it. For many, discovering the origins of my famous statements can be a "bitter pill to swallow" (also one of mine). To make this enlightenment easier, I will gently reveal the escapades that prompted me to make many of the statements you thought were probably made by others, perhaps Ben Franklin or even Shakespeare.

The origins of the above statement began with "Money is the root of all evil." This was first uttered by me at about age seven, during a brief socialist period, when my then five-year-old brother was routinely beating up a neighborhood kid who kept stealing his lunch money. After one bare-knuckle round was over, I commented, "Ed, that just shows you that money is the root of all evil. If we lived with no money, people would not fight." Well, someone overheard it, mentioned it to someone else, and within months it was worldwide.

About a year later, when my statement was already worldwide, my third-grade teacher instructed me to write an essay on "Money is the root of all evil." I was out of my brief socialist phase. So in thinking through this, I realized that without money I could not buy a new bicycle or clothes from some store other than Sears, where my dad got a 10 percent discount. Sears was not a cool place for a fashion-conscious boy to buy stuff.

So in my paper I wrote:

"The statement 'Money is the root of all evil' was obviously written by a wealthy person who wanted to discourage others so he could have it all. The truth is that the lack of money is the root of all evil."

My teacher must have mentioned my statement at a faculty meeting, because by the time I was thirteen, it, too, became known worldwide.

From ages seven to thirteen I was, frankly, precocious. Many of my comments on life were even made into advertising or political slogans. I never received credit or money. By age fourteen I realized that others were profiting from my commentaries, and so I shut up for a long time. With the publication of my first book, I decided to come out of the closet of anonymity and accept the credit for these statements. You will find many of my other statements in *Bartlett's Familiar Quotations*.

Look in the author section under "Anon."

You came into sales to sell, but it's not working out that well.

Perhaps you wanted to be a financial adviser and help people make their fortune (as well as your own, of course). You probably didn't think that most of your time would be spent searching endlessly for people with money. And worse, you had no idea that people with money wouldn't welcome your call, at least those few who haven't already signed up for the "Do Not Call" list. After all, you have ideas that should help people with money get a better return on their investments than they currently enjoy.

Or perhaps you sell business equipment. You have a degree in business and an outgoing personality, so you were drafted for sales. You would be taking home much bigger checks if only you had more face time.

Or you sell life insurance. If you can help one or two families each month protect their assets and provide for their families, you could make a very good living in the process. You found out in a hurry that most people don't want to talk to a life insurance agent. Not even in your most pessimistic brooding about your future did you realize it could be as bad as it really is.

The problem was driven home at your spouse's company Christmas party. You had been warned not to talk business, but in the back of your mind, you had an idea that people would at least want to know about some of the new life insurance products on the market.

Drink in hand, you bided your time. Then, as expected, someone asked what you did for a living.

"I'm a life insurance agent."

You might as well have said, "I stir the waste products at the sewage plant." The room couldn't have emptied out any faster.

Now, you certainly didn't come into sales to frighten or offend people.

THE PROBLEM WITH SALES IS PROSPECTING!

Where did all the prospects go? Are there just too many salespeople? Did something happen to scare them off?

Even worse than the shortage of prospects is that the longer you've been in sales, the more you hate prospecting. Why? They turn you down, reject you. Because they reject you, and because prospects are so hard to come by, you try harder and harder. And the harder you try, the more scared they get and the more you fail.

The major problem in sales is not really a problem with sales. It's a *prospecting* problem. The problem is scarcity. Most salespeople think there are not enough good prospects.

The reason you are reading this book is that *you don't have enough prospects*. If you had all you could handle, you certainly wouldn't be looking at a book on prospecting. Yes, I am very well aware that 99 percent of the salespeople in this country believe that rejection is the biggest problem. But that's not it. If you really believed that there were enough prospects for you to talk to, would you really care if some jerk hung up on you? Of course not. You'd move on to the next prospect. But since you and most other salespeople believe—consciously or subconsciously—that prospects are scarce, then rejection threatens survival. And that hurts.

Rejection is not the problem in sales. Nor is closing, a lack of product or service knowledge, too high a price, the "competition," or poor company advertising. The problem is scarcity of prospects. We live in a country of more than 300 million people. How can prospects be scarce?

In *Julius Caesar*, Shakespeare says, "The fault, dear Brutus, is not in our stars, but in ourselves, that we are underlings."

I say, "The reason for a scarcity of prospects lies not in the market but in our method." And that method is the one I call the Old Way.

THE OLD WAY OF SELLING

Every sales trainer I've ever had, plus all the books read and lectures heard, have focused on overcoming objections and on closing. J. Douglas Edwards, perhaps the best of what I call the Old Way trainers, preached that "half of your sales will be made after the prospect has said *no* six times."

In writing this book, I did a Google search for "overcoming objections." This particular Google search turned up 78,300 hits. I found this gem in the November 18, 2002, edition of *The Business Journal*, whose masthead says, "Serving Jacksonville and Northeast Florida":

"Psst—hey—com'ere. I've got a secret to tell you. Sometimes prospects will stall you, sometimes they will lie to you, sometimes they won't tell you the real reason they won't purchase. When a prospect gives you some lame excuse (stall) about why they won't buy now, he's really saying, 'not yet.'"

At www.entrepreneur.com, in "Overcoming Objections," March 27, 2003, we find these treasures:

"The prospect wants to say yes, but has limited funds."

Hmmm. What if the prospect actually wanted to say no?

"The prospect doesn't understand what you're saying."

Really? What if she does?

"The prospect has a difficult time making decisions, large or small. You have to help her decide."

Perhaps the prospect has in fact made a decision.

If we switch over to Amazon's search engine www.a9.com and search the text of books currently for sale, we find 535 books that include a discussion of "overcoming objections."

Regrettably, the Old Way is alive and well.

Concentration on closing and overcoming objections has defined a lifestyle for countless millions of salespeople.

This is not another book in that tradition, but I do think we should spend a few minutes highlighting the Old Way. Then you will understand what my system is not.

A wise young friend of mine named Bryan said, "It's just as important to know what you don't want as it is to know what you do want. Then you'll know what not to do in life." (Hey, I only hung out with smart kids.)

OLD WAY TEACHINGS

If you have been around sales more than one day, I am certain you have heard one or more versions of the three principles summarized below. I personally have no idea where I first heard them and doubt if anyone should be given credit. Here are the philosophical foundations of the Old Way.

- All buyers are liars. (Think I'm kidding? Do a Google search for "buyers are liars.")
- Don't believe the prospect until he or she has said no three, six, twelve, or twenty-seven times.
- Every no gets you that much closer to a yes.

As you can well imagine, if you believe these principles, they will affect the way you live. If you sell insurance, when you receive what the prospect thinks is a final no, you will press ahead anyway, thinking you are that much closer to a yes. If you are a financial adviser or planner and the prospect tells you he doesn't have any money now, you won't believe him but will charge forward anyway, ruining the prospect's day and your own when the prospect tells you which portion of the anatomy should receive your offer.

Most Old Way salespeople, consciously or otherwise, believe and act as if there is a war between buyer and seller. Your job as seller is to win! "We Shall Overcome" was not just the theme song of the civil rights movement. It's a song the sales movement has been singing for generations. It's one reason your approach usually isn't welcome. Too many generations of prospects *have been overcome.*

APPLYING OLD WAY PRINCIPLES

If you work in insurance, real estate, most financial services (except, of course, where my company does the training!), appliances, automobiles, or just about anything else, you have most likely been trained in the Old Way—*if you have had any training at all.* If you have had no formal training, you've still received the Old Way message. Like a powerful undertow, whenever you put a toe in the sales water, it's tugging on you.

Let's assume, for the sake of argument, that you are a salesperson in a financial services company. Perhaps you sell mutual funds and insurance. As I am sure you will recognize, the yarn I'm going to spin for you is all too typical. If you don't recognize yourself as the key player, I'm sure you know someone to whom this applies.

Assume you are fairly new in the business. Since you don't have any customers and therefore nothing else to do, it is abundantly clear that you have to prospect. Since you don't have much money to invest in mailings or seminars, you spend at least five hours a day on the phone. You would much rather wait for someone to call you or at least be provided with twenty or thirty direct-mail leads each week. But— as you quickly learn to your dismay—it doesn't work that way. Instead you decide to take the plunge one day when no one is listening. You sit down at your phone and start calling dentists, because after all they are people with money, right? After a half hour of struggling with receptionists, Dr. Jones answers his own phone. (As you know, this rarely occurs.)

Now, you happen to know that Dr. Jones has a huge practice. He and his spouse, Dr. Smith-Jones, drive his-and-hers Mercedes. This couple would, of course, be highly desirable customers.

Here's how the usual conversation goes:

YOU: [Ring, ring.]
DR. JONES: Hello.
YOU: May I speak with Dr. Jones please?
DR. JONES: Speaking.
YOU: Dr. Jones, this is Fred Smithers with Beam of Light Financial Services—
DR. JONES [interrupting]: Excuse me, but I am really not interested.

Before continuing with this now classic conversation, let's review your Old Way training.

First, you will undoubtedly have been trained to persist. In sales school, you probably heard countless anecdotes about how various superstar salespeople (also called "champions") have persisted and triumphantly returned with the prized order. In addition, your sales manager or your peers will have surely relayed some or all of these Old Way gems of wisdom:

- "No is a stepping stone on the way to yes."
- "No means yes later."

- "No is simply a misunderstanding by the prospect and is just a way of saying that he or she requires additional information."

With these philosophical pearls jangling loose in your purse or pocket, let's pick up on your conversation with Dr. Jones, who was saying:

DR. JONES: I am really not interested.

YOU: Of course you're not interested. If you had been interested, you would have called me, right?

DR. JONES [angrily]: I guess I would, but I didn't. So what does that tell you?

YOU: I understand you are not interested, Doctor. But let me just ask you this: what are you not interested in?

DR. JONES: I'm not interested in you. I'm not interested in Beam of Light Financial Services. But I'm very interested in getting back to my patients. I'm busy.

YOU: I understand you're busy. I find that most of my clients are busy, and it's for that reason that—

DR. JONES: [Click. Dial tone.]

YOU: [Sigh] [Addressing room at large] I wonder what I did wrong?

From the Old Way point of view, you certainly must have done something wrong. Weakness? Wimpy tone in voice? Failure to persist? Insufficient goal orientation? Bad phone breath? Sadly, you recall the words of Old Way trainer J. Douglas Edwards, who said that half of your sales will be made after the prospect has said no six times. So sitting there with a long face and a fly buzzing obnoxiously about the pizza crust on the table, you reflect on the magic number *six*.

"If only I could have gotten Dr. Jones to say no six times," you say to the fly, "I might have gotten his business. But," you say to the coffee cup with bits of creamer curdling on the surface, "Rome wasn't built in a day." (My statement, of course.)

And so you grind through another eight or twelve calls, and not one sale or appointment do you get. At the end of an hour, you feel as if you have been passed back and forth through a paper shredder. You're tired and discouraged.

Walking toward the door, you turn and make a rude gesture at a Post-it note on your phone reminding you to call Dr. Jones tomorrow and grind a few more nos out of him.

As you lock up, a terrible thought strikes. There was that videotape you saw in training. What was it the trainer said? Was it: "Don't believe the prospect until he has said no twenty-seven times"? It couldn't have been!

Poor you. You couldn't get Dr. Jones to say it even six times.

WHAT A WAY TO MAKE A LIVING!

I submit that the Old Way *is* one hell of a way to make a living. If you happen to be brand-new to sales and think I exaggerate that people are trained this way, go out and pick up most any sales book or attend a sales meeting almost anywhere.

If you would like to conduct your own tests of Old Way methods, by all means verify the following:

1. It is very hard on the salesperson. If you don't already hate prospecting, you probably will shortly by sticking to Old Way methods.
2. It is very hard on prospects. Why do you think the room empties out when a life insurance agent introduces himself? It's not the product. The product is really just a contract to deliver a known amount of money at an unknown future date. The problem is the sales method. After decades of nail-pulling selling skills, people have finally come to believe that a session with a life insurance agent will be unpleasant. And so it is.

But lest you think that this approach to sales is entirely without redeeming social value, it did serve its purpose at an earlier time in this nation's history. Undoubtedly it came of age in an era in which the old-time peddler could not make more than one call a day or even in a week. And in the old days, if you didn't sell on that one call, you didn't eat.

Today we live in an entirely different era of sales. Instead of being limited to one call a day, by using web conferencing software you can make a sales presentation in Bangor, Maine, at 9:00 AM and in Boca Raton an hour later. You can cover more territory by phone calls, letters, faxes, and emails in an hour than the old-time salesperson could in a month. In seconds you can blast out an email broadcast to prequalified clients and prospects. While you are wrapping up a sale or setting up an appointment, your personal computer can be cranking out twelve letters a minute. And who knows how many people can check your latest price quote on your company's web page?

It is a different world. And yet unfortunately, somehow, the old methods still persist.

This book is most definitely *not* about this Old Way style of selling. It's about what I'll immodestly call the Good Way.

THE GOOD WAY

The system of prospecting that I'm going to outline relies on three very basic assumptions:

The first assumption is that your product or service is sold, not bought. Millions and millions of people are obviously prospects for Frosted Flakes. But they don't get a personal sales presentation when they stroll down the cereal aisle. However, most people don't buy cars, financial services, real estate, insurance, computer systems, office products, or machinery often enough to buy these products without some help. Your job is to help people who might need complicated, sophisticated, or often expensive products, and for that, you need sales leads.

The second assumption is that there are enough prospects in your market area who are interested and qualified today to make it worthwhile to look for *them* and ignore the rest.

Let's take a close look at "enough." What would be "enough"? At least a few hundred. Suppose you sell promotional items to movie studios and there are less than a hundred of these. You would use a different strategy than I'm suggesting here. Each prospect is too valuable to take a chance losing.

By "interested" I mean *interested*. Ask a child, "Are you interested in ice cream?" The child's yes is the one I'm talking about. Ask the child, "Are you interested in going into the backyard and weeding the garden?" That no is the one that Old Way salespeople grind away on in their misguided efforts to convince the child that there is some remote benefit in weeding the garden.

By "qualified" I mean "has the capability to buy *now*." Your definition of being qualified will, of course, be different from mine.

Unless you have an extremely limited market, you can develop a simple way to look for those who are interested and qualified *now*. That's what a good part of this book is all about.

As you will see, in this book we're going to assume you don't have any customers. You don't know anyone. You've been thrown into a territory or a job, and it is gladiator-style fight or flight. (Mine, age eight.) You will use direct mail, web registration, phone, or some form of direct-response advertising to generate that lead.

There are ways to prospect other than those I will outline here. I'm referring, of course, to "relationship marketing," and it's clearly the subject of another book.

But now we're going to assume you are flying blind, that there are some people in your marketplace who need your product or service, and that it is possible to find them. You need to know how to find prospects who are interested and qualified *now*. Later I'll discuss whether you, the salesperson, should do the prospecting or whether you should get someone else do it for you.

The third and final assumption of the Good Way relies on the basic principle that not all buyers are liars. In fact, we'll assume the exact opposite; buyers tend to be truth-tellers.

The idea that buyers are liars is the fundamental assumption on which the Old Way is based. Old Way practitioners believe that if someone tells you they're not interested, what they really mean is "I need additional information." Or when buyers tell you "I don't have any money," what they really mean is "I don't have any money for that idea, but if you come up with another idea, of course I could raise the money."

I call this "translating English into English." And it assumes the prospect doesn't know his own mind or is spinning a lie.

If you treat people as if they are lying or don't know their own mind, you shouldn't be surprised if they don't respond well to your sales message. Undoubtedly, many people will lie to you, will create a smoke screen to tell you they're not interested when they are, or will rely on some other subterfuge to mislead you. Yes, their lies and smoke screens can be penetrated by Old Way selling. But do you *want* a customer list full of liars?

Remember the Golden Rule: do unto others as you would have them do unto you. Treat other people how you want to be treated. This rule works. It's been time-tested a lot longer than the Good Way. The Old Way ignores the Golden Rule.

You can build a selling system on one of two assumptions. First, you can assume, along with the prophets of the Old Way, that buyers are indeed liars. If you make that assumption, you must follow it with all of the various techniques to overcome opposition. You must be prepared to suffer endless rejection, and you must continue the endless process of translating English into English.

Or you can shed the Old Way and join the Good Way and make life almost infinitely easier.

THE GOOD WAY CAN CHANGE
YOUR SELLING LIFE

How you will live your sales life is about to change.

Remember Dr. Jones, who got the call from Beam of Light Financial Services? Here's how a practitioner of the Good Way would have handled it.

YOU: May I speak with Dr. Jones please?

DR. JONES: Speaking.

YOU: Dr. Jones, this is Fred Smithers with Beam of Light Financial Services—

DR. JONES [interrupting]: Excuse me, but I am really not interested.

YOU: Thankyouverymuch for your time. Have a great day. [Click. Dial tone.]

Thankyouverymuch, uttered as a single word, becomes the modern equivalent of *Hi-yo Silver* as you disappear into the electronic sunset of the telephone system in search of another prospect.

So let's abandon the Old Way and its tired, old methods and go in search of the Good Way.

You have been spending a lot of time and money on the Old Way, applying old philosophies of "throwing good money after bad." (Mine, perhaps one of my most inspired.)

But now it's time to adopt the Good Way of prospecting and "pick the cherries, not the pits!" Following this method, you will only throw good money after more good money.

Thankyouverymuch; it will be worth your time.

3

The Three Phases of Selling

The more things change, the more they remain the same.
—Bill Good, age eleven

On the face of it, this is an absurd statement. But when you understand its origin, you will see how it can be effectively used.

Beginning at about age seven, I was considered a slob, at least by my very proper, neat, orderly, Southern-raised mother. According to her, my slobbiness kept getting worse, not better. One day when I was eleven, she ordered me to clean up my sty, as she called my room. I was greatly annoyed by this order because I knew exactly where everything was. Instead of cleaning, I just moved stuff around. Stuff that was under the bed I put on the closet floor, and the stuff from the closet went under the bed.

When she made her inspection, she was furious. "Until you have a place for everything and everything is in its place, you are grounded."

I knew I had only once chance. "Mother," I said calmly, "the more things change, the more they remain the same." I could tell the wheels of her brain got no traction on that one. Of course it was absurd. But she started thinking about it. And then thought and thought and then left my room forgetting, as I had anticipated, to follow through on the grounding, whereupon I just put everything back where it was in the first place. And that is the true origin of yet another famous statement for which I received no credit.

I quote myself here because selling has been around at least since the second-oldest profession. And speaking of change, with this chapter, I am introducing some big changes for your selling life.

A completed sale will go through three phases before it closes:

Lead generation. In this phase, an individual, family group, or company is identified as having some degree of interest and possible qualification.

Once the lead has been generated, it must then be developed.

Lead development. This is the process of taking prospects with some degree of interest and perhaps uncertain qualification to the point where they are ready to seriously discuss purchasing your product.

Once an appointment is set with the salesperson, the sales process has begun.

Sales. In this phase, the salesperson goes through a series of steps intended to increase the prospect's desire to own the benefits of the product or service and reduce the fear of change. (Now, that's a really good definition of sales, isn't it?) When the desire finally seems to outweigh the fear of change, the salesperson ends the selling process with a close. Selling is the process of questioning, educating, persuading, overcoming obstacles, and then finally closing. Sometimes the prospect buys; sometimes not.

For the most part, this book will focus on lead generation and lead development.

LEAD GENERATION

Leads are generated principally from two very broad categories of marketing activity: relationships and mass marketing.

The only relationship marketing most companies undertake is to occasionally harangue their salespeople to ask for referrals. Salespeople, who hate asking for referrals almost more than they hate periodontal surgery, occasionally mutter, "You don't know anyone I could call, do you?"

This book focuses on marketing to people you don't know. We'll use the telephone and direct mail, and show you how both of these tools interact with a website designed for lead generation.

The point here is that lead generation is its own subject, its own skill set. It's the first part of what is commonly called "prospecting." Salespeople should not get anywhere near it, as you will see.

Once a lead has been generated, it must be developed.

LEAD DEVELOPMENT

As a rule, people who respond to a lead generation campaign or even those who are referred to you require some period of time getting to know you before they are willing to start the sales process.

These are your "pipeline" prospects.

Your pipeline (hopefully) consists of people who are moving toward a sale. Some pipelines are long. Some are short. "Pipeline time" could be defined as "the average length of time needed from the date of the first contact until a prospect becomes a client."

The lead developer manages most of the pipeline. The position requires someone with decent product knowledge, good communication skills, and the ability to answer many basic questions. The focal point of lead development is the point at which a lead is ready to be given a sales presentation. The tools that enable a lead developer to accomplish this are an important part of this book.

To some extent, a lead developer must take the point of view that he is protecting one of the company's most important resources: selling time. Sometimes, lead developers will only pass across leads that are virtually sold. When this occurs, the lead developer has, in essence, become the salesperson. This destroys the concept of lead development.

A lead developer communicates with a prospect *only* to the point where the prospect is willing to set up an appointment.

One way to tell if the leads have been developed appropriately is to monitor closing rates. Ballpark, good salespeople should close 50 percent of the properly developed leads they receive. If the percentage is too much below that, then there is a deficiency either in the selling skill or in the proper development of the lead. If the percentage is very much above that, then the lead developers are doing too much selling. It's a fine line and always a challenge to find the point at which a lead should be turned over to the salesperson.

SALES

Quite obviously, a good salesperson can take stone cold prospects and over the course of many hours develop them to the point where they will seriously consider buying your product or service.

But it is so much more effective, from a cost point of view, to use various marketing tools to generate a lead and then use someone *else* as a lead developer to move only the hot prospects into the selling cycle. Intuitively, you know these types of prospects. They get the blood pumping, enhance your focus, and overcome tiredness, even sloth. As we get further into lead generation and lead development you will learn how these two processes create what I like to call "more better."

WHY SALESPEOPLE SHOULD NOT PROSPECT

"You can lead a horse to water, but you can't make him drink." This is not my statement, because it is false.

According to me, "A good salesman can make a horse drink any day of the week." It works this way. A lead generator finds the horse. The lead developer then brings the horse to the watering trough, and the salesperson gets the horse to want to drink and gets him or her to drink.

Optimally, salespeople should not prospect. They should be supported by a team of people performing all the nonsales functions. I understand that many readers of this may be tempted to say, "Well, this is not for me. It's just me in the office. I can't afford a team."

Hold on.

Today you may be your own prospector, receptionist, computer operator, bookkeeper, and list developer. But to get big, you need a team. That is where we're heading. Wouldn't you rather spend your time in sales, and not doing all the other stuff?

Let's pose this question: if the salesperson is the one who makes the horse drink, what else should the salesperson do but that?

How about nothing?

There is a point in a salesperson's career, probably earlier than you may think, when he or she should not prospect. Not even a little.

I have known this for some time. People I have trained know it well. Now is the time for you to know this also.

The most valuable asset a salesperson has is time. It may also be the most valuable asset a company has, because as that famous sign that reportedly graced many General Motors dealerships said, "Until someone sells something, nothing happens." But just look at what different companies make their salespeople do!

Sadly, salespeople are required, sometimes in their job descriptions, to "service the account," attend countless meetings, and update databases, a task that can be filled by a typist. They are often expected to create monumental proposals, which can and should be crafted by someone else, if not by an entire department.

And, of course, salespeople are expected to prospect.

What a waste!

Strong words. But I'll back them up.

WHAT TO SELL?

Early in 1984, huge changes were hitting the financial services industry. At the time, my team of five seminar presenters were teaching rookie brokers in the United States and Canada how to prospect by phone. By then we had trained probably forty thousand of them, and I suppose if any single person should be blamed for the "Do Not Call" laws, it is me. Some months, we would do as many as fifty seminars with fifteen to forty attendees.

I knew I would have to adapt to the changes hitting the marketplace. I just didn't know what the changes would be.

A consolidation had started throughout the industry. Bache bought Thomson. E. F. Hutton disappeared into Shearson. One day Kemper Insurance bought seven regional brokerage firms. Each company had been a separate training account for my company but then they became one account. Talk about an income reduction plan!

I assumed the consolidation would continue, which it certainly has. I imagined that one day two giant firms would emerge, AGMerrillWebberWitterBrothers and FirstNationalCityWachoviaBankofAmerica. I further imagined I would have a training account with just one of these behemoths. However, following a change of leadership, a new training director would no longer require my services, and I would be out on the street, with a begging bowl in hand.

Since the begging bowl option was not to be a fork in my road, I decided that the best chance of survival was to produce something I could sell to individuals, not companies. There were, after all, a lot more individuals in the industry than companies.

The question was how I could replace the extremely profitable prospecting seminar I had developed. If the firms were not to be my major clients, then what would I sell?

One possibility was to put together an advanced sales training course.

Another possibility was to do something in the area of time management. But what?

Since I was not interested in letting the future of my company ride on possibilities, I decided that some serious research was in order.

I decided to start by figuring out what salespeople do with their time, a lucky choice if ever I made one.

TIME STUDY 1

My first attempt to find out what salespeople do with their time was to see if anyone else had done a study.

I had recently started writing for one of the major trade magazines in the industry, *Registered Rep*. I called and asked if they had any time studies. The answer was no, but my editor suggested I call some of the major firms.

My next call was to the assistant training director of Dean Witter. He was fascinated with the idea and urged that if I found the answer to share it with him.

My next call was to the training director at PaineWebber (now absorbed into the Swiss banking giant UBS—see what I mean?). Like my friend at Dean Witter, he was most interested in any results I turned up. He said he had heard that Quotron (the primary supplier of desktop information quote machines) was building a "work station of the future." At his suggestion, I called them.

They had no time management data but thought that the research chief of the *Wall Street Journal* might have something. So I called her. No, they had not done any such study. She suggested I check with some of the trade magazines. She suggested that *Registered Rep*. would be an excellent place to begin, whereupon I was right back where I started. As Dave Barry would say, "This is a true story. I'm not making it up."

I would have to do the study myself.

Since I was not an expert in time management, I took two courses. The first was from Hyrum Smith, who later became chairman of Franklin Covey, manufacturers of the Franklin Planner and later various software products to help manage time. The second course was from Charles Hobbs, who taught people who use a Day-Timer how to manage time. He subsequently sold his company to Day-Timer. In one of these classes I was introduced to a time log, a paper form on which one would write down each task, when it started, when it ended, and the kind of task it was.

The point of the time log was this: if you know where your time is going, you can control it. I figured that if I knew where brokers' time went, I might then discover an idea for a service or a seminar I could sell to them.

As soon as I was done with my second class, I called the local branch manager for PaineWebber and convinced him to let me do a time study with some of the brokers in his office. With his agreement, I spoke to some of his brokers, and after making my case to them, I recruited eleven people to participate in my study.

Early one Monday morning, probably in the fall of 1984, I met my eleven recruits in the PaineWebber conference room in Salt Lake City. I had adapted the time log to some particulars of the brokerage industry. After I explained how to fill in the logs, everyone assured me they would write down each task, noting precisely when it started and ended. I told them I would be back on Friday to pick up the results.

Well, that study lasted one billionth of a second. There was no way the brokers would take the time to fill out yet one more piece of paper. When I went in to pick up the time logs, most of them had some notes scribbled here and there, but these notations more resembled bird tracks than the hard data I needed.

Down in flames. But I was not giving up.

Time study 1 was a bust.

TIME STUDY 2

For a few weeks, I couldn't figure out how to do my study. One day I was standing in front of a RadioShack store and something caught my eye. It was a handheld computer with a tiny screen and a big sign that said, "4 K in RAM Memory!" I vaguely knew what that meant. To make a long story shorter, I bought the computer, and had it programmed so it would time and count things.

We had only enough memory to program the A to M keys. That meant I could track thirteen different categories of time. When a user pressed a particular key, it started a clock running. And it added a tick mark to its electronic counter. When the user pressed a different key, it stored the results from the first one, started another clock running, and added yet another tick mark, this time to the second key.

The results would give the total amount of time spent on any particular category as well as the number of times that button was pushed.

My original key assignments were:

A = incoming client service call
B = outgoing client service call
C = nonsales meetings—meeting with branch manager, sales meeting, training meeting
D = dialing and waiting on phone
E = talking to prospect by phone
F = meeting with prospect
G = talking about investments with client
H = meeting about investments with client
I = meeting with client or prospect in person
J = drive time
K = entering trades into computer, research, general preparation
L = investment research
M = turns it off

When one of the brokers in my study would take a call and realize it was an incoming client service call, he would simply press the A key. That started the clock and tripped the counter.

Next he calls a good client. The minute he starts the dialing, he presses the D key for "dialing and waiting on the phone." Once again, that starts the clock and trips the counter. When the client answers, the broker presses either G or B, depending on what kind of call it is.

At the end of whatever time period we are observing, we punch in a secret code, and the little computer tells us how much time was associated with each key and how many separate usages there had been.

At that point in my technological career, neither I, nor anyone working for me, had been able to figure out how to get data from a small handheld computer into a bigger one, where we could analyze it.

Instead we would write the results down and retype them into one of the early spreadsheet programs, Multiplan. With that data we could then produce charts, graphs, and consolidated reports.

My computer program was really quite fancy, and I had even impressed myself.

But before spending a couple of thousand dollars on handheld computers for the brokers in my study, I decided to be the first subject. So I made up the categories that I seemed to be spending time on and early one morning pressed the first key.

My study was under way.

My categories included things such as incoming call, outgoing call, staff meeting, writing, and administration.

At the end of the first day, I had confirmed that virtually the only thing I was finishing were the interruptions! As I recall, I had been attempting to write an article for *Registered Rep.* Instead of having one or two large blocks of writing time, there were well over a dozen short intervals. My concentration was splattered.

The killer was phone tag. I would sit down to start my article, and then someone I had been trying to reach for days would call. I would take the call and finish with whatever we were talking about. I would then return to my writing project. Then someone else would return my return of his return of my return of his return, and so on. I would take care of that. Then perhaps a staff member would need something. Once again, the concentration I needed was shattered. Once I saw the pattern of what I was actually doing throughout the day, it was abundantly clear why, at the end of the day, I felt not only tired but frustrated. I was not doing what I needed to do and was in fact doing things on other people's to-do lists. As a bonus, my concentration was subject to repetitive fracturing, a stress disorder if ever one existed.

Based on my personal time study, I immediately worked to change my business habits. I sat with my assistant and plotted out a strategy to use blocks of time for telephone appointments. That was really the start of what I call the model day.

We blocked off a period of time for writing, another for telephone appointments, and another for staff meetings and such.

My assistant's job description changed drastically. If there was someone I needed to talk with, she would hunt them down and set up a telephone appointment. And when people called me, if it was someone I wanted to talk to, she would set up a telephone appointment.

I was able to bail out of phone tag, surely one of the curses of the late twentieth and early twenty-first centuries.

Telephone messages were banned from my office, and today, twenty years later, you will not find one message.

With my day divided into blocks of similar activities, I began to finish what I started. At the end of the day, was I still tired? You bet. Frustrated over not finishing things? Much less, since I was actually accomplishing what was on *my* plan, and not the plans of others.

By the way, the model day for a lead developer should look something like this:

7:30 AM—Plan. This means get all the lists of people you will need to call today. Study the records of everyone you will be calling back, and make a note so you know exactly what you will be talking about.

8:00 AM—Make cold calls (assuming your marketing method requires them) or make first calls to the leads not yet contacted. Take a ten-minute break about every hour.

12:00 noon—Lunch.

1:00 PM–4:30 PM—Follow-up calls. These are your lead development calls.

4:30 PM–5:00 PM—Wrap up. Meet with the salesperson. Go over appointments set for the salesperson tomorrow.

TIME STUDY 3

When I saw the positive effects of knowing where my time went, I bought fifteen of what we came to call efficiency computers. I rerecruited the same eleven brokers at the PaineWebber office.

Once again I showed up early on a Monday morning. I passed out the computers and explained how they worked. And I told the brokers I would be back on a Friday afternoon to give them a secret code that would let them see where their time went.

This was in 1985, at the dawn of the computer age. My recruits were excited. They were part of a high-tech experiment. We had even programmed the computers to beep every five minutes just to remind them it was there.

On Friday afternoon, everyone showed up. I gave them the code, and they began writing down their results.

And as they began to write down the results for the M key, I heard a lot of mutter.

"Bill, this can't be right. It says I spent almost forty percent of my time in M, and you told us M turned it off."

Then they got it. I had told them the M key turned the computer off. But M was a key just like any of the rest. I was trying to see if we could figure out a way to count the time between productive activities. Actually counting the "off" time was the trick.

Here's what I found with this study:

Out of a nine-hour day, roughly four hours were spent "off."

Another two and a half hours were spent in service.

About one and a half hours encompassed a variety of actions that would cause a meeting or a phone call with the client or prospect to occur. These actions included drive time, dialing and waiting, setting up seminars, and general preparation.

Slightly less than an hour a day was spent meeting with and talking with interested, qualified clients and prospects.

I then did some "rocket-science mathematics."

The average broker in my study was bringing in approximately $240,000 per year in gross revenue. (The broker would get to keep about 40 percent of that.)

So I rounded that up to $250,000, which became, on average, a $100,000-a-year job.

I guessed that they were working about fifty weeks a year, and that meant they were bringing in about $5,000 per week.

And then it hit me:

These people are worth $1,000 an hour in gross revenue to the firm when they are meeting with and talking to clients and prospects.

This result was so shocking I did not believe it.

So I repeated my study over a longer time period in several different brokerage offices. I sent one of the computers to Bakersfield, California, another to Denver, and another to Clearwater, Florida. In each case we ran the study for three weeks.

And within a relatively small margin of error—10 percent to 20 percent—my results were the same. These brokers were worth $1,000 an hour.

The most interesting of the three studies was done with a broker in San Bernardino. He was averaging about $500,000 a year in gross revenue, and doggone if he was not spending about two hours a day with clients and prospects (five days a week × two hours a day × $1,000 = $10,000 per week × fifty weeks a year!).

This discovery—that "average" financial advisers were worth $1,000 an hour in gross revenue—caused me to immediately abandon my idea that I would offer some kind of advanced sales training.

When these folks are worth $1,000 an hour and only working about an hour a day, I realized that I had to come up with a way for them to have more of these $1,000 hours.

And obviously, all the other stuff they were doing—including "off" time—had to be replaced with sales calls.

No more prospecting, service, typing; none of it. Even someone with the IQ of a rock can see that you can hire people worth a whole bunch less than $1,000 an hour to do those other chores.

Now do you see why salespeople should not prospect?
Not even a little.

The Sales Assistant Study

Once I knew where the time went, I immediately started another study. I needed to figure out what sales assistants did or did not do.

In the brokerage industry, the term for the primary service provider was sales assistant. (Due to a sustained nag by me in my columns in *Registered Rep.* and later *Research* magazine, most firms today have adopted such terms as "client service representative" or even "client service manager" to let people know who to call for service.) With a broker's time worth $1,000 an hour, it seemed like the sales assistant was key.

As an aside, I always found the position of sales assistant an oddly named position. You would think the position would help someone sell. Not so. The sales assistant is actually the person who primarily does client service. A sales assistant might serve one or several brokers (now called advisers).

My research started with my friend the local PaineWebber branch manager.

I asked him, "Could I see a copy of your sales assistant job description?"

I might as well have asked him for the design specs of an atomic bomb.

I was more than surprised to learn that there was no such document. With no job description, the term "sales assistant" was just a free-floating job title. A sales assistant was whatever a person who had a sales assistant wanted that assistant to be.

Mostly the assistants did client service. But I knew of brokers who had tried, mostly unsuccessfully, to get their sales assistants to cold-call, set client appointments, or even set up seminars.

I was extremely interested to see if advisers could use this assistant to delegate not only client service but also to get help in selling.

A little later that same year, I made a most unusual arrangement with the local branch manager. I hired a sales assistant for his branch. Since I paid her salary, we agreed I could also manage her and she would report back to me.

My objective was to discover a way to use the sales assistant position to maximize the time the adviser would spend meeting with and talking to clients and prospects. Obviously I couldn't just tell the adviser "You're spending too much time in service. Stop it."

No, service has to be done—but, I thought, not by the adviser.

In the process, I intended to produce a sales assistant job description so that people who hired a sales assistant would know what the assistant is supposed to do.

We experimented with different ideas. One idea was to structure the day so my sales assistant did client service in the morning and made calls to clients and prospects in the afternoon. That was a complete failure. Every time we tried it, an incoming call would hit and blow our outgoing campaign right out of the water.

We tried to set up smaller time blocks throughout the day. That failed.

No matter what we did, I could not structure the day so that a sales assistant could do anything other than client service for more than a few minutes.

Finally, after failing consistently for some months, the heavens opened and one of those epiphany moments occurred. The person performing client service *cannot also cold-call, set appointments, and get people to the phone*.

We need a different person!

THE SALES SUPPORT TEAM

Based on my sales assistant study, I concluded that the full support team would be at least two people. But there was still a lot I didn't know.

I visited big-producing offices in the Salt Lake City area over several days. I talked to advisers and staff. I wanted to know how much work it takes to produce $1 million of gross revenue a year.

A $1 million producer is always a top dog and receives much praise and attention, in addition to $400,000 or more in income per year.

My studies led me to believe that it took 120 to 140 hours a week to produce $1 million a year.

I realized that no one makes it to the big time without a team. And if people say it is possible, they're lying through their teeth. Or they are working sixteen hours a day, seven days a week. They're on the fast track to a heart attack *and* a divorce.

I also realized that a sales professional needed two arms: a client service manager to take care of service, and a sales assistant (that person who helps him sell) to keep the calendar full. After the "off" category from our time study, service and prospecting were the two biggest categories of broker time.

I had that nailed by 1986.

There was still one more piece.

COMPUTER OPERATIONS

In December 1986, I incorporated these ideas into what I now call the Bill Good Marketing System. I told my few clients that they needed a sales assistant and a service assistant and maybe a computer operator.

I said, "If you can type, save yourself the money and type in your own notes."

But within just a few weeks of launching my system, I sent out an urgent message:

"Get a computer operator! No exceptions!"

Why?

Even from advisers who could type eighty words per minute, I saw major mistakes in data entry. I saw them over and over.

After a lot of conversations, I concluded that advisers *in a sales frame of mind* would mess up a computer system as surely as birds fly. And to the extent that they got into a *computer operator frame of mind,* they could barely sell.

So the $1 million support team became:

1. full-time service assistant;
2. full-time sales assistant; and
3. part-time computer operator.

How Does This Apply to Me?

Let's assume you sell widgets or s'mores or something.

How much are you worth per hour selling your product and actually meeting with clients and prospects?

How much time a week do you spend doing that?

How much time doing all the other stuff?

You get my point?

While I discovered these principles in financial services, they apply to *any* sales profession where you sell a reasonably big ticket item. Exactly how you implement the support team can vary. The principles do not. Specifically, these immutable laws most certainly do not change.

THE IMMUTABLE LAWS—
FROM A POSITIVE PERSPECTIVE

1. Salespeople should sell. At an hourly rate approaching $1,000 when actually selling, it is absurd to do anything else.
2. Sales assistants (also called prospectors, lead generators, lead developers, callers, qualifiers—the name doesn't matter) fill the salesperson's calendar with interested, qualified clients and prospects to talk to and see. Depending on the operation, a sales assistant might do lead generation and lead development, or just lead development.
3. A client service assistant (if not an entire corporate service department) must handle all client service problems, manage the office, and protect the salesperson's time.
4. A computer operator handles all data entry, proposals, letters, faxes, and emails.

THE IMMUTABLE LAWS—
FROM A "DON'T DO IT" PERSPECTIVE

Violate any principle and there are penalties. If the following laws are broken, the penalties are severe—and always happen, sooner or later.

1. Where sales support and service support are performed by the same person, service will inevitably squeeze out sales support.
2. Where sales support and computer operations are performed by the same person, computer operations will instantly expand and consume all available time, thus causing the immediate disappearance of sales support.
3. Where service support and computer operations are performed by the same person, service support will gradually disable computer operations, causing them to vanish. Except in an emergency and for a short period, one cannot combine an administrative position with a people position.
4. Where a salesperson is performing all of the above duties, you get low productivity and a mess.

A MESSAGE TO MANAGERS

If you are managing one or more salespeople, where do you start?

You can start almost anywhere. We typically start with computer operations. Get your salesperson off the computer.

Then handle service.

Now fill your salespeople's freed-up time with more prospects by bringing on a sales assistant.

THE CHICKEN

One of my most famous and shortest lectures is just two words: "The chicken."

Those two words answer the ancient philosophical question "Which came first, the chicken or the egg?"

Various philosophers have postulated answers to this question.

The ancient Greek Heraclitus said, "It was the chicken, and in a related development, the egg."

The Eastern sage Attila the Hun said, "It was the larger of the two that determined which came first."

But the Western seer—now living quietly in Utah—issued his pronouncement with a slight smile: "The chicken."

There—someone finally answered the question. You feel better now, right?

Here's how it applies to you.

Put the chicken in place before you get the egg. Don't think for a minute, a millisecond, or even a nanosecond that you and your sales team can ratchet yourselves off a plateau by sheer hard work alone. Once the dreaded plateau sets in, that's it for you unless you put the chicken in place. If you say, "We can't afford any help at present production levels, so we'll have to work harder and pull ourselves up to the point we can afford some help," my answer will be, "The chicken comes first." Get a cash advance on a credit card and hire someone, if only from eight to noon. Buy some selling time. Create the chicken—whoops, I was about to create a new famous statement when I already have one—oh, earlier I said it was the goose . . . but whatever . . . to lay the golden eggs.

The chicken comes first.

FOCUS ON TIME

Since I learned the value of a salesperson's time, my entire focus in designing marketing and prospecting systems has not been to make salespeople better in selling. Rather, it has been to help them spend more time selling in front of better qualified clients and prospects.

Part of our strategy is this: someone can be hired to generate leads for just two or three times minimum wage. So let's get these high-producing salespeople to delegate some portion of the prospecting process by hiring it out. You don't like lead generation or lead development? Chances are you are worth hundreds or thousands of dollars an hour, and you know in your heart of hearts that when you spend time prospecting, you are taking a huge pay cut. This is certainly one of the real reasons for the so-called call reluctance.

If you're a high-producing salesperson or if you manage one or more high-producing salespeople, consider solving your prospecting problem by hiring someone specifically to do some part of the process. Naturally, their first course would be to read this book. Their first action would be to master lead generation, turning over all leads generated to the salesperson. As skill level increases, the lead generator can start making the follow-up calls and move into lead development.

By the way, even if you know you are worth $1,000 an hour, you need to master prospecting once and for all. Ultimately you will have to teach your assistants how to do it. If you can't do it, you will hire someone less skilled than you, and your pocketbook will gush.

There are at least three separate skill sets normally required for success in sales. You have to be good at finding the horse (lead generation), getting the horse to water (lead development), and good at making the horse drink (sales). I have seen great salespeople fail because they can't find any leads. With no leads to develop, they get no hot prospects into the selling process.

Always remember: "Salespeople should sell"—soon to be yet another famous statement.

You read it here first.

4

The Good Way
to Prospect

Show me the money.
—*Bill Good, age twelve*

This statement is attributed to Cuba Gooding Jr.'s character in the Tom Cruise movie *Jerry Maguire*.

> JERRY MAGUIRE: What can I do for *you*, Rod?
> ROD TIDWELL: It's a very personal, very important thing. Hell, it's a family motto. Now are you ready? Just checking to make sure you're ready. [Rod turns his boom box real low.] Here it is—show me the money. [He now blasts the boom box at full level.] OHHH!!!! SHOW! ME! THE! MONEY! Doesn't it make you feel good just to say that, Jerry? Say it with me one time brother!*

The true origin of the statement, however, is this dialogue with my mother:

> FRANCES GOOD: Bill, I promise I'll get your allowance for you today.
> BILL GOOD: Mom! You've been promising for days. My income is a very personal thing. So here it comes. SHOW! ME! THE! MONEY! TODAY!

* http://en.wikipedia.org/wiki/Jerry_Maguire.

She was amused with my formulation, and when she went to the mid-week meeting of the ladies' Bible class at our church, she mentioned what I had said. By the time I was thirteen, it was worldwide. Cameron Crowe, the screenwriter and director of *Jerry Maguire*, obviously plucked my statement out of the ether, dropped the last word, and got paid millions. All I got was my $2.25 allowance. Life isn't fair (also one of mine, age fourteen).

This is not a book on telemarketing. It is a book on prospecting and lead development. Nevertheless, one must pay attention to the "Do Not Call" laws. Let's suppose you generate a lead from a homeowner. Further suppose that this person has registered his or her phone number with the "Do Not Call" website. You have ninety days to turn them into a client, or get written permission to continue calling, or you must quit calling. The telephone is one of many tools to generate leads. However, it is a critical tool in developing them. So many examples will refer to it.

Now that I've given the Old Way a severe blow, I had better offer something in its place.

The remainder of this book is designed to replace the tired, worn-out way of prospecting, which in turn will change the way people sell.

This chapter contains the new rules of selling that replace the exhausted principles of the Old Way.

PROSPECTING

Frequently in my training seminars I ask all the trainees in the room to close their eyes. I then say, "Create a picture in your mind of a prospector." When I see they have done that, I then ask, "Open your eyes and tell me what you saw." Most people report seeing an old man with a mule, a pick on his shoulder, and a big pack on the back of the mule. Well, we're going to talk about prospecting in exactly the same sense as that old gold prospector.

A decent dictionary definition of the term "prospecting" is: "the act of searching for something of value." And that is exactly what the old gold prospector did.

Once gold was discovered in California, people came by the millions, because gold had been found there. They didn't stop in Fort Lauderdale or detour through Rio de Janeiro or Easter Island. They were heading for gold-rush country! When they got there, they looked for certain geological signs that told them gold might be found in one spot rather than another. Among the things they looked for were deposits of black sand—heavy, iron-based sand. If there was any gold to be found, it would be mixed with that sand. After the old prospector staked his claim, he would shovel the sand into his pan, and from that point on, his primary interest was getting rid of the dirt. Gold prospecting was and still is *primarily the act of discarding what is not gold*. The prospector gets rid of such things as dirt, grit, gravel, mud, and twigs. Assuming there is gold in his sample to begin with, the more nongold he discards, the more gold he finds.

So if the Good Way has historical roots, they are in the California goldfields and not with the old-time peddler. In Good Way prospecting, the first thing you do is: disqualify nonbuyers. The Old School sales trainer counsels various techniques that enable the salesperson to hang on to anyone who will speak with him or her. But the Good Way prospector says, "If it don't glitter, it's dirt and out it goes."

So what then are we looking for?

The Four Qualifications

The "glitter" we're looking for is composed of the four qualifications. These exist in greater and lesser degrees. At least two of them *must be present* before you put someone into your prospecting pipeline.

Interest: This is the first thing we look for. If Dr. Jones is not interested at all in Beam of Light Financial Services, the other qualifications *do not matter*. He is not a prospect and must not go in our pipeline.

Decision: The person you are talking to is the decision-maker or is minimally on the team.

Time: Available now or later.

Money: Available now or later.

If you get your mind set to disqualify people who do not have the right mix of these characteristics, and if you actually disqualify them and move on, you will nearly fall out of your clothes when you find your first real prospect who is interested.

Good prospects are located, not created. Locating enough good prospects who are ready to act, while also developing those who are not immediately ready to begin the sales process, is the first key to sales success.

This is the entire focus of lead generation.

THE FIVE PRINCIPLES OF THE GOOD WAY

The Good Way to generate leads is built from five principles:

1. When generating leads, whether you are cold-calling or calling a warmer list such as advertising responses, when a prospect says "I'm not interested," believe him. Politely hang up and find someone who is interested.

   Even when the prospect appears only *marginally* interested, move on.
2. You can contact (call, mail, email) a list of prospects (people you believe to be qualified to own your product) more than once if you don't rough them up with Old Way methods.
3. Continue contacting a list as long as it is profitable. That could be months or even years.
4. Select a limited market and seek to dominate it totally by staying on message.
5. By improving your lists, as will be discussed in chapter 12, you will improve your market to the point where you have achieved domination.

Let's explore these five principles in greater detail.

The First Principle of Good Way Prospecting

Here is a thought experiment for you.

What effect do you think you would have on people if, instead of attempting to keep talking to everyone you talk to, you tried to get rid of them?

How would you react?

While you're pondering your answer, let me tell you where I burned this lesson in my own mind. You will have a similar experience when you implement this first principle. This goes all the way back to the cassette tape era.

I had decided to experiment with different ways to promote our public seminar, which at the time focused solely on telephone prospecting. Salespeople in many industries were invited. Some of our programs were geared to the specific needs of a single company or industry, but the public seminar is one that virtually anyone could profit from.

The idea went like this: "I wonder if I can send out a cassette tape of my sales presentation, get various sales managers to play it for their crew, and get some of them so excited that they would show up at a seminar. By doing that, I won't have to make that same presentation over and over and over."

It sounded like a good idea to me, so I made twenty copies of a cassette tape, prepared some written material, and then one morning sat down with our local newspaper, cut out some ads that contained phone numbers, and started calling. (I've always liked calling people who pay money to publish their phone numbers. They tend to answer the phone on or before the third ring.)

One of the first people I called was the local representative of a very well-known sales training course. I figured it would be quite a score to sell them a prospecting course.

The conversation went like this:

ME: Mr. Jones, this is Bill Good with Bill Good Marketing. We specialize in training salespeople to find new business by phone. Tell me, is the telephone at all important to you as a marketing tool?

MR. JONES: Well, yes. It is.

ME: Very good. We're having a seminar on February 9 in the Salt Lake Hilton. We have prepared a free cassette tape that will tell you all about it. Would you like to receive a copy of this tape?

MR. JONES: Well . . . you can send it out if you want. We would probably listen to it.

ME: Well, Mr. Jones, it sounds to me like you have everything under control there. Since this tape costs us $1.52 to get out the door, if you don't mind I'll just pass at this time. So thankyouverymuch. [Click. Dial tone.]

Now, there probably isn't one of you reading this book who would have just tossed Mr. Jones out of the gold pan as I did. Where there's life, there's hope, right? (I made this statement at age eleven when a friend said, "My mom is hopeless!" Not realizing she was being sarcastic, I replied, "Where there's life, there's hope." Someone overheard it and mentioned it to our preacher, who used it in a sermon. The rest, as I said later, is history.)

So why did I hang up on him?

I hung up on him because he was *not interested enough*! I knew I could probably have sold this man a seminar ticket, or perhaps several. But I also knew that to do it, I would have had to first send him the tape, then call him back six times before he would play it for his salespeople. And then I would have had to call him back another three times to find out how many people would be coming to the seminar.

I also knew that I could take the same amount of time I would have spent with him, call rapidly down my list, and find someone who was *very interested* in attending one of my programs.

Yes, I know it's possible to sell people who are initially not interested. But your time is much better spent by letting those disinterested prospects go while you look for someone else who is very interested. There is no shortage of good prospects!

When you find someone who is interested in your product, the relationship goes so much more smoothly that it makes sales a joy, rather than the agony of tooth extraction that many sales trainers have made it.

The first principle of the Good Way is: When a prospect says, "I'm not interested," believe him or her. Politely hang up. Go find someone who is interested. Where the prospect appears only marginally interested, move on.

Be careful here. I am talking mostly about the lead generation phase of the entire sales process. Once you have been talking with someone and are moving him or her through the lead development process or have even started into sales, you would certainly try to find out why the person is no longer interested and then handle *that*, if possible. But if you are making a first contact on a cold list or even a warm one, such as trade show leads, follow this principle and find a prospect who is interested *now*.

The Thoughts Behind the Words

According to me, "Actions speak louder than words."

Obviously, verbal communication means words. But in our first principle, we added a physical action. I tossed him out of the gold pan. That enormously increased the power of the communication.

Let's look at the *complete* communication I delivered to Mr. Jones.

When I withdrew my offer to send the tape (action) and told him I felt he had everything under control, I delivered another communication as well.

Didn't I tell him that unless he was really interested, I wasn't?

Didn't I also tell him I had all the business I could handle?

Didn't I place value on my tape by making it scarce?

Suppose I had taken the flicker of interest he showed and just jumped down his throat?

What would my actions have said about my product? Wouldn't my actions have said, "This is hard to sell. So just show me a glimmer of interest, and we're going to the mat"?

What did I say when I told him that I was not going to send him the tape because it cost $1.52? Didn't I tell him—by my actions—that he was worth less than $1.52? And finally, what did I say when I just hung up (politely, of course)? Didn't I say, "Listen, Mr. Jones, there are a lot of people out there who would love to know about this program. So while you're sitting there thinking about it, I'll find them and you'll miss out"?

In short, I delivered a big package of communication to Mr. Jones in just a few politely spoken words. To put power in your words, use just a few words and communicate the rest of the thought with an action.

After all, actions do speak louder than words.

The Second Principle of Good Way Prospecting

The story of Mr. Jones is obviously incomplete as it now stands and, of course, it has a happy ending. Here is what actually happened.

When I'm testing a marketing idea, I do what we call Stage I testing. I normally write a letter, fax, email, and/or script. Depending on the campaign, I will then make the calls myself to see if it works. These can be client calls, cold calls, or calls to people who hit our website. I work out any bugs I find and then, when I can make it work, I turn it over to someone else in my organization for Stage II.

In Stage II, a person I have trained makes a lot of phone calls to see if my initial results continue to hold true. In this case, I turned the test over to Jill Olsen, who was then my assistant and is now the president at Bill Good Marketing, Inc.

At this point in our testing, we weren't too concerned with finding out which prospect list was best, so Jill just grabbed the Chamber of Commerce directory. She started calling, and before long she managed to encounter the same Mr. Jones I had spoken with on the first day of my test. The conversation went like this:

JILL: Mr. Jones, this is Jill Olsen with Bill Good Marketing.
MR. JONES [interrupting]: Are you the folks trying to give away that tape?
JILL [no clue where that remark comes from]: Yes, we are.
MR. JONES: I want one.

Needless to say, this time he got a tape. And sent two people to the course.

Our second Good Way principle is: You can contact (call, mail, email) a list of prospects more than once if you don't rough them with Old Way methods.

The Third Principle of Good Way Prospecting

Our second principle raises a question, doesn't it?

How many times can you call or mail to the same list?

To answer that question, let's talk for a moment about our friend the gold prospector.

Now, this old codger went up into northern California, found himself a claim on a pretty stream, and dug a couple of ounces of gold right away. At the end of the first day, you can suppose that he had a tough question to answer: "What shall I do tomorrow?" Well, if you were the gold prospector, you would answer, "I think I'll stay right here." Two ounces of gold a day is definitely profitable. How long will you stay there? Until all the gold is gone? I wouldn't.

Let's say that you have been prospecting that stream for six months. You average half an ounce a day in that same spot. Would you stay there or go look for a better claim?

The answer depends on the alternatives, doesn't it? You may hear that upstream they're taking out two ounces a day. Your risk is: stay for a sure half ounce a day, or risk losing that and go for the big strike. Which do you do? It depends on how much risk you want to take, doesn't it? Let's say you stay another month. Now your claim is producing only an ounce a week. At this level it costs you more in supplies than you are making in gold. So naturally you head upstream.

It's the same with a prospect list. Let's say you call or mail to a list and get a profitable response. Recycle the list!

Our third principle of the Good Way states: Continue prospecting a list as long as it's profitable. That could be for months or even years.

As a side note, I am frequently asked, "How long should I leave a person on the list?"

My answer is: don't second-guess the list. When the list is no longer profitable, throw the whole thing away.

The Fourth Principle of Good Way Prospecting

Ultimately you want to dominate your market. You will do that by first selecting a limited market. Unless you are Wal-Mart, no one wants to deal with a company named "Everything for Everybody."

So focus on some part of the total market.

It needs to be big enough to support you and unified in some important way.

Example: My company focuses on the development of marketing systems that enable our clients to have the time and the money to pursue their goals outside of work.

We don't try to have a list brokerage firm. We don't write brochures for people.

We develop marketing systems.

What do you do?

The answer to that question is the message that you must drive into the minds of the individuals in your market.

So to dominate a market, you need to select one. And you have to have a message to communicate to that market.

Let's use the term "brand" to refer to the message you are going to communicate to your chosen market. Your brand is how people recognize or remember you. It's how they separate you from all the other planners, dentists, or widget enhancers in the market.

The essence of your brand is a statement of who you are.

Do you hold yourself out to be a financial planner—along with four hundred other planners in your community? That's a tough assignment.

Perhaps you should position yourself as a "financial craftsman." Does that stand out from the crowd? A Google search turned up only three of them.

Do you "sell investments"? Yeah, you and five thousand other advisers.

So perhaps you specialize in "helping plan the final third of your life."

Imagine the confusion you would experience if you saw an ad in your local newspaper featuring a picture of your mailman giving a seminar. Stunned, you look closer and see he is giving a seminar on real estate investing. "Does my mailman know anything about real estate investing?" you seriously wonder.

I certainly don't want to learn that my orthopedist does brain surgery on weekends. I don't want my dentist having a part-time widget business.

This issue of having a message—a specialty—and staying on message is vital to market domination. Without a message, you have no tool to drive into the minds of the individuals who comprise your market.

Fortunately for me, I don't have to spend much time on this except to refer you to the pioneering works on branding by Al Ries and Jack Trout. They wrote originally as partners but now write separately.

Here are my strongest recommendations:

1. Read *Positioning: The Battle for Your Mind* by Al Ries and Jack Trout. This will help you understand how to get your message heard above all the clamor. In a word, it's about how to claim a piece of mental real estate. *Positioning* is available and in print as a twentieth anniversary edition. Order it immediately.
2. Next read *The 22 Immutable Laws of Branding* by Al Ries and Laura Ries.
3. Then read *Differentiate or Die: Survival in Our Era of Killer Competition* by Jack Trout.

With the invaluable know-how from these books, you can create or even fine-tune the message you must deliver countless times.

Our fourth principle is: Select a limited market, and by staying on message, seek to dominate it totally.

That principle is, in good measure, the secret to small business survival. You may not be the biggest fish in the ocean, but you certainly can be the biggest in your market.

The Fifth Principle of Good Way Prospecting

The stepping stone to dominating your market is improving its responsiveness to you.

It's easy to talk about markets.

You can improve a market, dominate it, blah blah blah.

For the salesperson or sales team, a market is a list of individuals or companies with whom you have decided to have a business relationship.

Giant companies live in markets. Individual salespeople—even when working for giant companies—live with their lists, which usually are a tiny piece of a giant market.

Your market is your client list, your prospect list, and your mass-market list, often called a prospect list.

I'm going to assume you have some mass-market lists. We will talk later on how to develop and refine these lists. But for now, let's just assume you have some lists of people in the market you want to dominate.

To improve response you have to improve recognition through what I will call the list improvement techniques. They are:

Repetition

It has been said that the three main laws that determine the value of a piece of property are location, location, and location. Well, the three main laws that determine recognition or familiarity are repetition, repetition, and repetition.

Major firms obviously use the principle of repetition. On any TV miniseries, you'll see the same ad four to six times per night. Some companies, such as American Express, McDonald's, and Coca-Cola, run with an ad for years.

De Beers has been running "A diamond is forever" since 1948.

Avis has been "trying harder" since 1953.

You've been able to "Be all that you can be in the Army" since 1981.

If large corporations and governments spend hundreds of millions of dollars repeating the same ad, don't you think it might make sense for a salesperson, with a limited market of perhaps fifteen hundred prospects, to do the same thing?

Whether you call, mail, show up at trade shows, or drive people to your website with a clever direct-mail campaign, you must get repetition working for you.

How does the small sales team implement repetition?

If you have a campaign that works, keep doing it.

Rule of thumb: Someone once said, "It takes at least six times for a person to hear your name before he or she will remember it." True? Maybe. But it's definitely more than once. So be on the safe side and commit to a promotional campaign unless it is a complete flop.

I have known people who mailed the same list fifty or more times.

One of my clients cycled through the same list for twelve years. It kept working. He never bothered to change it.

Make it safe to communicate

Repetition can also hurt you or even drive you out of business.

Once again, assume you sell widgets.

You get a list of five hundred widget users and pound on them using Old Way techniques. You trick screeners into putting you through and *never* take no for an answer.

According to me, you will wear out your welcome. By pestering and hounding people, you learn that repetition really does work.

YOU: Hello Mr. Jones. This is Ralph Bucket with Beam . . .
MR. JONES: [Click. Dial tone.]

Through your actions, you must convince the list of people you want to do business with that it's safe to communicate with you. How? Simple. When the prospect says, "I'm not interested," you say, "Thankyouverymuch." Click. Dial tone.

After a while, people will come to believe that it is safe to talk to you. They will understand that you won't jam something down their throats. At that point you will find you are no longer making cold calls. You will be finding people who are at least willing to talk.

Create interest

YOU: How do you know if a prospect is interested?
ME: Early on, willingness to talk. Requesting info, asking questions. As you near the point where you should close, the prospect will almost always ask questions.
YOU: How does one create interest?
ME: You start out by finding someone who already has a base level of interest. They typically answer yes to an interest question, such as "May I send you a report outlining why widgets will reduce the average homeowner heating bill by twenty-five percent or more?"

With a base level of interest established, you increase it by showing how the benefits of your product will help your prospect achieve some positive goal or avoid a negative action.

"If I could show you how our widgets could also save you thousands of dollars of repair bills to your furnace, would you give me a half hour?"

Many salespeople confuse talking with selling. They think that if they can talk on and on about the features of the product, sooner or later the prospect will hear something that sparks interest and decide to buy.

It's not the features that create interest. It's the benefits. A benefit is what the customer actually buys. Hardly anyone cares about the antifriction reduction factor in a widget! But that's what salespeople talk about on and on and on.

And as you blabber on, you are slowly sucking the life out of the sale, just not perhaps in the way you might think.

Here is probably the reason why salespeople talk about features: while the prospect doesn't really care about the product features, they ask questions about them. Salespeople, who have been asked about countless features, think this is what the prospect is buying and so blabber on.

People buy benefits, not features. However, they ask questions about features, not benefits.

Why?

To prove to the salesperson they are analytical buyers, not emotional pushovers.

If you cover all the features, the prospect won't know enough to ask questions. And mostly, if they cannot ask questions, they will not buy.

Based on a lot of experience, here are the facts as I have learned them:

1. When you get near the close, to prove something to the salesperson, most prospects feel they must ask questions.
2. Mostly the questions will concern features, not benefits. By asking about features, they believe they can convince the salesperson that they are sophisticated buyers.

   Examples:
   Automobiles: Does the stereo come with antitheft protection?
   Mortgage: What is the grace period?
   Mutual fund: How long has the manager been with the fund?
   Dishwasher: Do I have to rinse the dishes before I put them in the dishwasher?

3. If the salesperson has meticulously covered all the features, the prospect may not be able to think of an intelligent question.

4. Therefore, since the prospect cannot think of any questions, and since he or she needs to ask questions, he or she may not buy.
   Blabbermouth!

So to create interest, focus on benefits and withhold features. It is imperative that you do this in your phone calls, emails, letters, and faxes.

Encourage word of mouth

Yes, you have to have a great product and great service to generate the best of all advertising, word of mouth. But if you also have a list on which word of mouth can occur, look out!

This principle was very important in building my business.

In 1978, I advertised a seminar in the *Los Angeles Times*. More than seventy people showed up, among them a broker from E. F. Hutton as well as some agents and a district manager from Farmers Insurance.

After the seminar, I followed up. I sold in-house seminars to Hutton and Farmers. Using a list of branch managers from each company, I just went from one to the next.

These people know each other and know each other well! They go to meetings together frequently. They call each other. They help each other.

So I started calling and writing. From 1978 to 1980, my trainers and I taught approximately five thousand Farmers agents. In 1980 I did more than eighty prospecting seminars for Hutton. From Hutton I went to Dean Witter, then on to PaineWebber, etc. In financial services, it's a small business—as it is in your market.

Even if you work for GE, you have a limited market. The same is true for Microsoft. The people selling small-business servers have a defined market. You have a tiny piece of that.

In my case, I got lists on which word of mouth was possible. By getting satisfied clients to write me letters telling me what a great seminar I gave, I spread the word of mouth to people who also talked to each other and met periodically in sales meetings.

So our fifth principle of the Good Way is: Through the four techniques of list improvement, improve your market to the point where you have achieved domination.

To summarize: At any one time, a prospect is located, not created. Over time, through repetition, by making it safe to communicate, by creating interest, and by encouraging word of mouth, good prospects can be created and the market dominated.

THE OLD WAY REVISITED

By now you see there is a certain truth to the Old Way, which I have retained.

When someone says "I'm not interested," the Good Way says "Thankyouverymuch." But we call or mail again . . . and again . . . and again.

In Good Way prospecting, we take only one no at a time. The Old Way will take as many as it can get on one call. By using the Good Way, you can go back, and over time you will come to own a given market. And if you are really astute, you will note that we just took the Old Way, spread out the nos and voilà! It became the Good Way.

So let's move on and talk more of good prospects and where and how to find them.

5

Lead Classification by Temperature

If you don't know the words, you can't sing the tune.
—Bill Good, *age nine*

For a while, I was in the boys' choir at the First Presbyterian Church in Greensboro, North Carolina. We were rehearsing some hymn or other, and the director asked, "Why aren't you singing?" I replied, "I don't know the words." He said, "Try anyway." I said, "Sir, with all due respect, if you don't know the words, you can't sing the tune." I was soon booted out of the choir because a bunch of kids started just humming along. We could have started an early fad as "The Hummers." They didn't know the words, either. But the choir director took my statement *and* blamed me for being a troublemaker.

The terms that follow are so critical I have reproduced them for you in the Prospect Action Cheat Sheet. You can get your own copy from the chapter 5 download page. The password for this chapter is cherriesandpits. You might want to get the cheat sheet now. If you have not yet registered, now would be an excellent time. You will need to first log on to the site. Then, as you will find, each chapter with downloads has its own password.

The Prospect Action Cheat Sheet won't make complete sense until you read chapter 24, "Lead Development Messages." Nevertheless, as you read this chapter, refer frequently to your cheat sheet. You will want to take plenty of notes, too.

The documents I am making available on the website for this book are intended for people who bought my book. I'm well aware that you can give the password away, but the documents won't make much sense without the book. In addition, you will be cheating your friends and acquaintances out of the knowledge they will gain from studying this book. So instead of giving away all the passwords you discover reading the book, why don't you just tell them you loved the book and they really should buy one? Deal?

Thankyouverymuch.

Now let's talk about classifying prospects.

If I say the term *hot prospect,* you have a pretty good idea what I mean.

It's what you live for, right?

Well, if there is a hot prospect, there's certainly a cold one. Surely there are gradations in between.

So we're going to use the idea of a thermometer to guide us in our prospect classification.

Let's define a prospect as someone who has responded to a lead generation campaign or who has been referred to you and with whom you would like to do business.

Here's another important term: *track.*

Track refers to the sequence of actions taken when you get a new prospect or when you upgrade or downgrade one.

We will use an ABCDE classification system, where each letter stands for a category of prospect. ABCDE are designations you can easily use in any database to track, sort, and prioritize prospects.

PROSPECT THERMOMETER

There are five categories of prospect, which you will meet shortly. Each has a place on your prospect thermometer. Additionally, there are people in your database who are no longer prospects because they bought your product and became clients. Let's just say that clients have a temperature of 212°F.

At the very bottom of our scale are ill-tempered folk we wouldn't accept as clients for any amount of money. Their temperature is −459.67°F—absolute zero.

We're interested in what's in between.

A hot prospect is 150°F.

At 0°F, you will find people who have no interest whatsoever. They cannot even be called prospects according to our definition. They are what I like to refer to as pits.

Between 0°F and 150°F are three other prospect types: red cherries at 120°F, green cherries at 90°F, and info leads at 60°F.

Let's start at the top of the thermometer and work our way down.

THE HOT PROSPECT

A hot prospect is a decision-maker (or on the team) who is very interested and willing to begin the sales process.

Characteristic	The Test to See if the Characteristic Is True
Interested enough to begin the sales process	Sets an appointment, preferably in person or by phone. Setting an appointment is *the test* of whether they are interested enough to be classified as hot.
Financially qualified	Comes out in conversation, by research, or by asking directly.
Decision-making capability	Verified by asking directly.

Appointment = hot. A hot prospect is not quite ready to buy, so the water's not boiling yet. The temperature is up there, but it will take a skilled salesperson to further heat the prospect to boiling.

No appointment = not hot. There is a way of testing the water to see if someone who might be a hot prospect really is.

For example, let's say you sell accounting software for dentists.

You are talking to a prospect, Dr. Phil D. Payne, D.D.S. He is a referral from another dentist. You believe you may have a hot prospect.

YOU: Dr. Payne, I recommend we get together in your office. I'll demonstrate our software to your staff and answer any questions you may have. In that way we can see if our program and your needs are a good fit. I have a spot open Thursday afternoon at two. Would that work for you?

DR. PAYNE: That would be fine.

Good. Hot prospect.

Now what are you going to do with him?

Well, take a peek at your cheat sheet. Look at the section called "Track." This is how you will handle *all* hot prospects.

But what if he's not hot? Instead of agreeing to the appointment, suppose the conversation takes this turn:

DR. PAYNE: You know, Mary Jane, I really need to think this over. Can you call me in a week or two?

Let's pause this conversation for a second.

We tested to see if Dr. Payne is hot. In this example, he is clearly not.

To find out if you have a hot prospect, verify financial and decision-making qualifications and then *ask for the appointment.*

No appointment = not hot.

But he's not cold, either.

What is he?

Let's do another test.

YOU: Dr. Payne, let me ask you one quick question. What is the one thing you most want to improve in the way you manage the finances for your practice?

DR. PAYNE: I want to be able to get data to my accountant early in the year so tax preparation is not a last-minute emergency.

YOU: We have a white paper called "Instant Tax Reporting." It will explain how to have the data ready for your C.P.A. by January 15. If I send that to you, and if you like what you read, would we have a basis to continue this conversation?

DR. PAYNE: Absolutely.

Let's run this conversation one more time, this time as if you were an Old Way practitioner.

First of all, as an Old Way salesperson, you would never have volunteered to send anything to a prospect.

In your training, you had this gem drummed into your head:

> You mail, you fail.
> You mail, you fail.
> You mail, you fail.

Your Old Way conversation would have gone like this:

YOU: Dr. Payne, many of my clients like to take a few minutes to think things over. And what I would suggest you do is think it over for the next hour or two. Jot down any questions, and I will see you in, say, two hours at your office. Would that work, or would three hours be better?

DR. PAYNE: I am not ready to meet with you, and as a matter of fact, I *hate* pushy salesmen. Go pester someone else in two hours. [Click. Dial tone.]

You, as an Old Way practitioner, have now fouled your own nest.

But you, as a Good Way prospector, have left the door wide open and perhaps intrigued Dr. Payne with your low-key approach.

When you determined he was not hot, you dropped down the temperature scale and tested the next lowest notch.

RED CHERRIES

That next notch down the thermometer is a red cherry. These folks almost glow in the dark, but they're *not* smokin' hot.

A red cherry is a prospect who is *currently* interested enough to receive literature from your firm, who has the funds now to purchase your product or service, and who is able to make a decision or is on the decision-making team. A red cherry is not currently interested enough to set an appointment. Many red cherries will, however, become hot prospects as long as you don't try to barge into their home or office before they are interested enough to start the sales process. It's the lead developer's job to get them interested enough to set an appointment.

Here are the red cherry characteristics and tests:

Characteristic	The Test to See if the Characteristic Is True
Interest	Talking, asking questions.
	If neither: offer literature, as follows:
	Make a statement and then an offer that firms up their interest level.
	Statement: I have a white paper that will show you how to get your taxes to your C.P.A. by January 15.
	Offer: If you like what you read, would we have the basis for continuing a conversation?
Decision-making capability	*Ask directly:* Are you the top dog in the decision-making food chain, or would we need to consult with your boss?
Time	*Ask directly:* Ask for a commitment to review the material: If I send this out to you today, would you have time to look it over by next Friday?
Money	Comes out in conversation, by research or asking directly.
	Ask directly: If you like what you see, our accounting package runs $14,000. Would that amount be a problem at this particular time?

I am going to spend a fair amount of time discussing red cherries for the simple reason that they are probably the most common type of prospect. If you fail to understand that their flicker of interest needs to be fanned gently, you will lose them. You know that. You yanked a few of them into an Old Way presentation and saw that interest vanish like a lover's whisper when you pushed too hard.

Testing for a Red Cherry

Let's look at another example of testing to see if we have a red cherry.

We *always* start with interest. If the person to whom you are speaking is not interested, *nothing else matters*.

How do we find out if someone is interested?

You are talking to them in a pleasant manner about your product or service.

Or better, they ask questions: "How many armadillo burgers are in the starter pack?"

Or you make an offer and ask if they would look at some literature:

YOU: For restaurants of your size, we have an Armadillo Burger Starter Pack designed to introduce your customers to the no-fat advantage of this unique food product. May I send you some information on our frozen armadillo burgers as well as a sample for your own use?

The answer we want is yes. But we'll take no and move on.

If interested, we next qualify for decision:

YOU: Is there anyone else on the decision-making food chain right there at the Roadkill Café?

And, of course, we determine time availability.

YOU: If I send this out today, you should receive it by Thursday. Will you have time to cook up a few armadillo burgers by, say, Monday?

And then the big one: money. Unless you know with a high degree of certainty, you ask.

YOU: If you like the idea of armadillo burgers as a menu choice for your restaurant, would you be able to invest $2,000 for a starter pack?

Again, the correct answer is yes.

Will some people lie to you?

You bet! But we are going to assume that our prospects are truth-tellers. So even if we know they have money when they say they don't, we'll believe them.

Before your red cherry prospect morphs into a hot prospect, you will have to deal with their questions, issues, requests for additional information, references, and so on. If you try to set an appointment too soon, red cherries can cool off quickly.

Old Way Red Cherry Picking

A prospect says, "Send me something." This is a plain English statement. The Old Way high-IQ salesperson translated that into another plain English statement: "He's afraid and wants me to provide additional benefits and close again."

This goes on all day long:

Prospect statement: We wouldn't be interested in armadillo burgers.
Old Way translation: I don't know anything about the "no fat" benefit. Can you explain it to me?

Prospect statement: Most of our customers are vegetarian.
Old Way translation: A small minority of our customers eat meat and might well be interested in your burgers.

Again, this is the Old Way technique of "translating English into English."

It takes a massive IQ to do this all day long.

That's why I sometimes refer to my method as the "low-IQ approach." Most salespeople try to make things too complicated. The only possible explanation is that their IQs are too high.

Therefore, one of the benefits of reading my book cover to cover is that I will lower your IQ 20 to 60 points. When your IQ is lower, life is much easier.

> PROSPECT: Can you send me a couple of samples of your armadillo burgers?
>
> GOOD WAY PROSPECTOR: Suppose I send you an eight-pack. We'll send them FedEx on dry ice. I'll have them to you on Friday. You try them over the weekend and see what your family thinks. Fair enough?

And then, of course, qualify for decision, time, and money. Examples of qualifying questions:

FINANCIAL SERVICES

Interest: Mr. Jones, would you like to see some information on the growth strategy I am recommending?

Decision: I would imagine you and Barbara would both be involved in the decision-making process, correct?

Time: If you like this strategy, is there anything happening somewhere else in your life that would keep you from making a decision in the next few weeks?

Money: By the way, I am accepting accounts now for investors who have accumulated at least $250,000 or more. If you like our strategies, is it fair to assume that we could continue with our conversation?

COMMERCIAL REAL ESTATE

Interest: Have you given any thought to increasing your real estate holdings?

Decision: Would you need to consult with anyone else on a decision to buy additional properties?

Time: If I came up with a perfect property for you, is there any reason why you would not have the time to look at it closely?

Money: If you did find a building you liked, do you have the cash and credit to handle, say, a $3 million mortgage?

COMPUTER SALES

Interest: Would you like to look at some information on the new free-floating, gravity-resistant network server we just got in?

Decision: Who else would need to sign off on a new server?

Time: If you and other members of the Technology Committee like this new server, is there any reason why an evaluation couldn't be done in the next couple of weeks so a decision could be made?

Money: Lease payments probably wouldn't run more than $400 a month. If you like the idea, could you handle that?

Developing a Red Cherry Prospect

YOU: Okay, Bill, I've got a bunch of red cherry prospects. What do I do with them?

ME: If at all possible, you develop them into hot prospects.

YOU: How do I do that?

ME: The short answer is: Follow up when you say you will. Provide additional information as requested. Ask lots of questions. Answer their questions and provide references as requested.

YOU: How do I know they're ready to turn over to a salesperson?

ME: They sound very interested. A prospect may ask very specific questions, such as, "How many armadillo burgers in a box?" At that point you say, "I want you to spend a few minutes with my partner. She's been here a lot longer than I have. Let me introduce you to Susie Hammer; she is available now. Hold, please, and I'll transfer you over."

If hot prospects are 150°F, red cherries are 120°F or so.

Ideally, red cherries and all prospects less than hot belong to lead developers, not salespeople. (Salespeople sell, remember?) And when a hot prospect is no longer hot, he or she goes back to the lead developer to be reheated.

Messages to Red Cherries

When you promise someone information on your product, you need to send a letter, an email, or even a fax.

Depending on the circumstances of your contact with a red cherry prospect, you will send one of four messages, each of which is included in the lead development messages you will obtain from the chapter 24, "Lead Development Messages," download page. All of these messages are summarized in the Prospect Action Cheat Sheet. Each of the red cherry messages sends the requested information. Which one you choose will depend on how the person became a red cherry, your prior relationship (if any), and who called the prospect (you or your lead developer). To understand exactly how to use all the lead development messages, you will have to read chapter 24, "Lead Development Messages," download them, adapt them to your market, and use them.

GREEN CHERRIES

Let's go back to our conversation with Dr. Payne.

Let's assume you've asked him if the white paper "Instant Tax Reporting" can provide the basis for continuing the conversation.

DR. PAYNE: Absolutely. However, I must tell you that we will be moving our offices in two or three months and I could not possibly implement a new accounting system before then.

Hmmm. Now what?

He's not hot, as we expected initially.

And he's not a red cherry because our definition specifies that a red cherry is "currently interested."

So let's see what kind of prospect we've got.

YOU: I completely understand, Dr. Payne. Moving your office has to be worse than an hour or two of dental drilling without Novocain. So let me suggest this: Suppose I put you down for a call three months from today. In the meantime, if I come across some further information on how our software might improve your practice, especially getting ready for tax season, I'll send it to you, okay?

DR. PAYNE: Yes, that would be fine.

YOU: Let me just confirm a couple of details we have covered, okay? Our software will provide complete insurance, Medicare, and Medicaid billing, which you indicated was vital to you, correct?

DR. PAYNE: Yes, that would be essential.

YOU: And we agreed that a $14,000 purchase price was in line with other programs you had investigated and that if you like what you see, that amount would not pose a problem, correct?

DR. PAYNE: It would not be a problem, I assure you.

YOU: One last item and I'll let you go. If you will give me your email address, I will shoot the "Instant Tax Reporting" white paper off to you.

DR. PAYNE: PhilDPayne@PhilDPayneDentistry.com.

YOU: Thank you very much. I'll call you three months from today. [Click. Dial Tone.]

So what kind of prospect is he now?

Again, he's not hot. He's not a red cherry. He's interested. He has the money but cannot act now. He is the decision-maker.

We call this second type of prospect a green cherry. There are actually two different ways to classify a green cherry.

The first is simply called a green cherry.

A green cherry is a prospect who indicates interest but who will not have either the time, the ability to decide, or the money available until some known later date.

The second type of prospect is a green cherry–conditional opportunity. Consider:

DR. PAYNE: I'm not sure when I can deal with this. My wife and I have been invited to a wedding in Rome, and we will take a few weeks' vacation after that to tour Europe.

Hmmm. He's interested. He's qualified. But we don't have a date when he could decide.

In financial services, you see this all the time:

INVESTOR: We've decided to sell the beach property and invest the funds for some additional income.

Once again, our prospect is interested and qualified, but the beach house has to be sold first. So we're missing a date, which is why this prospect is "conditional." For him to become a full-blown green cherry, we need that date.

With a new green cherry, we will send three letters: one today, one in two weeks, and another two weeks after that.

As you will see in the Prospect Action Cheat Sheet, we have a different strategy for dealing with a conditional opportunity greenie than with standard green cherries.

We send some information now but schedule calls in two-, three-, or four-week intervals to touch base and find out if our client has received an offer on her beach property.

In either case, the Old Way practitioner would have just hammered away:

OWP: Dr. Payne, many of my most successful clients overcome adversity, such as vacations, and have allowed us to install the accounting software in their absence. Why, we have even had people install it in the midst of tornadoes and hurricanes. So I'll be right over with . . . blah blah blah.

Green cherries can be among your best prospects . . . if you stay in touch.

Their temperature is 90°F.

We'll talk later about the formula for keeping your name alive between now and then. And greenies, of course, belong to the lead developer.

INFO LEADS

An info lead is a very important lead. Many leads actually start here.

An info lead is a prospect who requests information, but we know little else about this person. At the time the lead is identified, we don't know if they are on the decision-making team, are financially qualified, or even if they have the time to pursue the matter now.

They are typically generated in one of seven ways:

1. Call in
2. Fax in a reply
3. Mail in a reply
4. Registration at your website
5. Cold-call lead who says "Send me the information" and will not be further qualified
6. Referred in
7. Card dropped in trade show booth

Here's how Dr. Payne might have started:

YOU [on a cold call]: This is Susie Hammer with Acme Accounting Software. You know who we are, correct?

DR. PAYNE: Yes, I see you every year at the national dental conferences.

YOU: Dr. Payne, we have a new report available on how to have your numbers ready to go to your C.P.A. no later than January 31. Could I send you a copy?

DR. PAYNE: That would be fine.

YOU: Excellent. I will have it out the door today. If I send it today, you should receive it by Thursday. Will you have time to look it over by next Monday?

DR. PAYNE: I'm not sure. Just send me the info. I have to run. If I like what I see, I'll call you.

The same scenario can roll out on a website registration. Someone registers and takes the free info, but you don't know anything else about them. You certainly can have trouble catching up with these leads.

An info lead is 60°F. When people refer to warm prospects, it's generally an info lead they have in mind.

Important note: The info lead category is for new leads only. You would never downgrade a higher-grade prospect to this status. If they have been a lead before based on information you already know and then they say, "Just send me the info," I would probably consider them a cherry, or I might downgrade all the way down to pit and be done with them.

PITCH-AND-MISS

Let's pick up our conversation with Dr. Payne three months later.

YOU: Dr. Payne, Susie Hammer with Acme Accounting Software. We spoke three months ago, and as promised, I'm calling you back after your vacation. I trust you had a wonderful trip.

DR. PAYNE: I guess. But I have another problem. Both of my assistants are moving out of state. My bookkeeper had a beehive fall on her, and I have decided for now to stay with our current software. It doesn't do everything I need but it does get the job done.

It looks like we're nowhere, right? Well, almost.

He's not hot. He's not a red cherry. And now our green cherry who seemed interested has fizzled out.

He's a pitch-and-miss. You swung and missed. Sometimes you will be defeated by circumstances, sometimes by competition, and sometimes by that ancient bugbear fear of the unknown.

By pitch-and-miss I mostly mean a prospect likely spoken to several times and with whom you wanted to do business. The salesperson may have made a full-blown presentation, probably including profiling, preparing a written proposal, even asking for the order. Some or all of that occurred, but the sale didn't happen. Oh, woe!

In some cases you can pitch a red cherry or a greenie who stopped returning your calls or said no. In such case I would certainly try to get them to agree to be on your mailing list.

I will tell you this without any hesitation at all: If this prospect is someone you regret not doing business with, keep the name. Put him or her on the pitch-and-miss track. And over time, you will get a substantial percentage of pitch-and-miss leads turning into red cherries, hot prospects, and then clients.

At my company, approximately half our business comes from people who previously turned us down!

When you pitch someone, you still have a prospect, don't you? He is someone who responded and with whom you want to do business. These guys are 50°F.

On the Prospect Action Cheat Sheet, you will see what we're going to do with him.

Grading Your Prospects

Let's give our prospects each a grade that corresponds to their temperatures.

A = hot	150°
B = red cherry	120°
C = green cherry	90°
D = info lead	60°
E = pitch-and-miss	50°

NONPROSPECTS

(and the Sixth Principle of Good Way Prospecting)

There are a couple of nonprospects you need to know how to deal with.

At exactly 0°F, they are pits.

Pits are not interested. They have no warmth and certainly no love.

They just are. They really are mass-mail names. You might make your offer and most likely they say, "I'm not interested." They're not cherries. They're pits.

Pit defined: Anyone who is uninterested, unqualified, and/or unable to decide.

> YOU: We have a sample pack of armadillo burgers I would like to send you at no charge.
> PIT: We have no interest in armadillo burgers.
> YOU: Thankyouverymuch for your time. [Click. Dial tone.]

As you can imagine, someone can be a pit on initial contact or can descend into pitness.

What do we do with pits?

We return them to the list from which they came. I would not waste any time documenting their pitness. Just toss them back in the pond.

If you are like most salespeople, you have an intimate knowledge of pits, because you spend the bulk of your prospecting time doing what I call pit polishing.

As an activity, pit polishing is singularly unrewarding, consisting as it does of talking to, grinding on, and applying Old Way skills to people who are not now interested or qualified. It is virtually impossible to create interest on a single phone call or appointment. Pit polishing is the single biggest destroyer of salespeople that exists.

So here is the sixth principle of Good Way prospecting. Study it well: Pits are seeds. They sometimes grow into cherry trees. That's why we leave them on the list as long as the entire list is profitable.

At −459.67°F (absolute zero), we have a unique species: jerks.

These are the nasty, hostile people you run into from time to time.

When you encounter them, you need to mark them in your database somehow so you know to never mail or call them. There is only one reason for keeping these people, and that is so you won't accidentally get them back if you type in or import a new list.

In our database we have a field called communication status. A choice in that field is perm off.

When we import a list, we can identify duplicates. And if we find M/M Jerkus on the list, we can delete the new entry, thus ensuring that one does not slither back into our lives.

Here is what I am sure you would like to do to the next jerk you run into:

YOU: [Ring, ring.]

DR. JONES: Hello.

YOU: Is this Dr. Jones?

DR. JONES: Yes, it is.

YOU: Dr. Jones, this is Jane Smithers with Beam of Light Financial Services.

DR. JONES: Are you trying to sell me something? Why, you have your nerve, calling me. Who is your manager?

YOU [banging phone on table three times]: Did you hear that sound?

DR. JONES [alarmed]: Yes. Is there something wrong with the phone?

YOU: No. That was just opportunity knocking. [Click. Dial tone.]

If you find that a little strong, try this:

DR. JONES: Are you trying to sell me something? Why, you have your nerve, calling me. Who is your manager?

YOU: Oh, no. I'm not selling anything. I was just calling to tell you that you are the beneficiary of a very large . . . [Click. Dial tone.]

Okay, okay. I got carried away here. I'm really not recommending that you do this. Jerks are very few and far between. Yes, I have hung up on them from time to time. Maybe only four or five times over a long career in sales. Don't confuse the point here with the drama of its expression.

The point is that under the system I am teaching you in this book, *you* are the rejector, not the rejectee. If in doubt as to whether a particular prospect is a pit or a jerk, always remember that good manners are good business.

Still, when you encounter one of these people, just get off the phone as quickly as you can and move on to the next.

So these are our prospects and some nonprospects as well.

ASSIGNMENT

1. If not already done, download the Prospect Action Cheat Sheet. Print and study it.

2. If you want to download the lead development messages, you will have to read enough of chapter 24 to find the password.
3. Even if you don't have everything operational, start classifying your prospects ABCDE.

6

Advice to Cherry Pickers

Since the beginning of time, sales trainers have preached to their sales crews the importance of a positive attitude. Frankly, a positive attitude isn't really necessary to be a cherry picker. What you do need is a "don't care" attitude. Imagine you are sitting on an assembly line. Every minute an item drops out of a chute for you to inspect. It's either a hot prospect, a cherry, a green cherry, an info lead, a pitch-and-miss, a pit, or a jerk. Your job is to quickly test it and then, depending on what it is, drop it into another chute. Do you care if it's a cherry? Not at all. Just as long as you know what it is.

This don't-care attitude is crucial to cherry picking. Here's why:

People like doing business with professionals. A professional doesn't get emotionally involved in whether he or she will succeed. The professional knows that if the right actions are taken, anticipated results will follow. No big deal.

Furthermore, professionals will have arrived at a point in their careers where they have all the prospects they need. If they had any more, they wouldn't know what to do with them. This abundance communicates to the prospect, who realizes that it is the prospect who must qualify to do business with the professional; this is why the don't-care attitude is so important.

In other words, the art of assuming the correct attitude is the art of acting like a professional before you may actually be one.

THE CHERRY PICKER'S METHOD

Much of the remainder of this book will be a detailed expansion of the method outlined below. Basically, you have the method and then its organization. Both are equally important. I am giving the method here, in summary form, so you can begin practicing its concepts as you go about your work.

1. Find a good list. (We'll have lots to say about this!)
2. Generate some leads. Contact the list in a low-key, nonoffensive manner. You can call, mail, get them to your trade-show booth, or even drop by. Pluck off the hot prospects, cherries, green cherries, and info leads. Leave the pits on the lists. Don't even bother to write down "not in," "not interested," and so on. You'll be recontacting them, and they may well be interested at that time. Do not prejudice your list with negative comments.
3. Develop your leads by phone, supported by letters, faxes, emails, and materials from your website.
4. Contact your prospecting list again in forty-five to ninety days. Once again, remove from it the prospects that are hot, red, and green. Follow up with each according to the correct track.
5. Continue calling or mailing to your same list as long as the response rate you get from it is profitable and compares favorably with the response rates available on other lists. You will determine this, of course, by keeping track of the campaign statistics.

The Cherry Picker's Way of Life

Cherry picking is a very pleasant way of life for a salesperson.

If someone is not interested, neither are you.

If they're unpleasant, don't deal with them. Look for people you would like to do business with.

And when someone isn't interested, just utter the cry of the cherry picker—*thankyouverymuch*—and move on to your next call. Not all your cherries will pan out. Or as the old prospector might once have said, "Everything that glitters ain't gold. But if there's no glitter, for sure it ain't gold."

BOOK TWO

Lead Generation

7

Welcome to the "Do Not Call" Era

If your clients are people you contact at home, you need to read this chapter very carefully.

For you, there are two keys for sales survival in the "Do Not Call" era:

1. You must know the rules and be able to prove that you are abiding by them. It is not enough merely to abide by them. You must be able to prove it. This means that when you check numbers on the DNC website, you keep copies of print screens to prove you are attempting to follow the law.
2. You must have a strategy for prospecting that does not require cold-calling a residential list.

Here are the facts:

1. The national "Do Not Call" laws restrict both interstate and intrastate solicitation calls. This means that any person, anywhere, who has registered with the "Do Not Call" Registry cannot be solicited at the registered numbers without written permission or first responding to some solicitation or becoming a client.
2. As of August 2007, 143 million telephone numbers were registered with the "Do Not Call" registry. There are not a lot of residential or cell phone numbers left. The American public told us, loud and clear, "Don't call me!" There will always be a few procrastinators, but do you really want them as clients?
3. You can solicit people with business listings. If you are not certain whether a number is a business or a residential number, check the

Yellow Pages. If a number is in the Yellow Pages, it should not be registered on the DNC site. You can legally call it.

4. You can call clients who are registered on the DNC site *if they have made a transaction with the seller within the past eighteen months* unless they have specifically told you "Do not call me." In this case, you must respect their wishes and not call. It's the law.

5. You may call people who are registered on the DNC site *if they have made an inquiry with the seller within the past ninety days.*

After ninety days you can continue to call prospects at home, as long as they give you written consent. This has no set expiration, but it must (a) be in writing; (b) be signed by the person being called; and (c) include the number you are allowed to call.

And emails don't count. *Get it in writing.*

Based on the pervasive fact that the "Do Not Call" laws exist and are being enforced, we believe you should adopt them as your guide to socially acceptable behavior. When 143 million people scream "Don't call me!" it doesn't take a genius to realize you probably shouldn't call people at home.

If you are in an industry that requires contact-at-home phone numbers, such as home improvement, home construction, investment, and insurance, then you must meticulously gather written consent forms.

The person who gets the written consent will get the client.

On the website for this chapter, we have some sample forms and letters. These have been run past our attorney. You will, nevertheless, need to check with your own counsel before using these documents. The password is consent.

8

Introducing Lead Generation

If you go to Answers.com and search for "another kettle of fish," you will find this entry: "A very different matter or issue, not necessarily a bad one. For example, 'They're paying for the meal? That's a different kettle of fish.' First half of 1900s." That's almost correct. The true origin is 1958. So the entry from Answers.com should have read, "Second half of 1900s."

I used to feed my cat, Midnight, in a little kettle. One night she was really hungry. I fed her two kettles of fish. My mother said, "She ate another thing of food?" I replied, "To be precise, that was another kettle of fish." Our family came to refer to "another kettle of fish" as something different from what was originally said or thought. As it spread outside the family, it just came to mean "something different altogether."

The sales process consists of three broad phases:

1. Lead generation
2. Lead development
3. Selling

A lead generator will find a person who meets certain minimum qualifications. Sometimes these are red cherries or green cherries. Occasionally a hot prospect will leap up. Most times, the lead developers cull through the people who throw their card in a trade show fishbowl or hit your website. Lead generators are the first line of defense for the salesperson's time. They find the names of people with some amount of interest and qualification.

Lead development consists of contacting these leads by phone, email, mail, or fax with the intent of upgrading them to the point where they qualify as *hot*. When so identified, hot prospects are turned over to the sales department to begin the sales process.

FOCUS OF LEAD GENERATION

Lead generation can be broken down into two very broad categories: mass marketing, and relationship marketing.

Mass marketing deals with people you don't know.

Relationship marketing, which is another kettle of fish, deals with people you do know. We will not deal with relationship marketing in this book.

In some industries—financial services, for one—someone with lots of relationships might never make a cold call, conduct a seminar, or stand in a trade show booth.

THE PLAN

Mass marketing for an individual salesperson or small business is really not "mass marketing." More properly it should be called "micro marketing," because the markets we're dealing with are small.

Our marketplace is certainly not the 13 million small businesses just in the United States, as it is for Microsoft.

It's a tiny piece of that. But the principles we're going to apply are some of the principles the big guys also apply. We'll stick with the term *mass marketing*.

Here's the plan:

We are going to step through developing a campaign. You will need the collateral material I've put on the web for you. By the end of book 2, "Lead Generation," you will have created your own campaign and will hopefully try it out.

We are going to master each part. So no fair skipping ahead.

9

Campaigns

The Variables

The phrase "open a can of worms" is thought to be Canadian, from about 1955. It's actually American, about 1955. We were going fishing, and I had picked up a lot of worms that crawled out on the sidewalk after a rainstorm. I put them in a spaghetti can that normally contained my brother's favorite food. The poor boy was hungry. He picked up the can and stuck his fork in it. "Ed, no!!" I screamed. "It's not spaghetti, it's a can of worms! Don't open the can of worms! Gross. Yuck." He dropped it like a hot potato (also mine), spilling my worms. "Open a can of worms" went on to mean to introduce an unsavory subject into a conversation. As nearly as I can recall, there was a Canadian family camped nearby. They undoubtedly overhead me screaming and started telling their relatives when they returned to Canada . . . which fully explains why so-called experts would assume this is a Canadian statement instead of finding its true source, me.

It's time to dig in. (Mine.)

I have organized the process of lead generation into campaigns. A campaign is a series of steps or actions, taken in a given market, that produces predictable results. For example: You send out flyers in newspapers promoting free nose piercing for your line of jeweled nose rings. Every time you send out 10,000 flyers, you get 150 to 200 phone calls.

You have a campaign! It involves a series of steps that can be repeated in a given market with predictable results. Whether you are making a profit in the nose ring business is not the issue. A campaign has to produce only *predictable* results to meet our definition of a campaign. Since your results are predictable, you have a campaign.

But let's assume that most of the calls are from outraged parents telling you which anatomical portion can receive your nose rings. Okay. Let's change something—say, the publication. Instead of sending your flyers out in the regional edition of *The Christian Science Monitor,* you switch to a heavy metal magazine. Now you get two hundred calls, and these are all from kids wanting nose rings.

What changed the result?

You changed a *variable.*

VARIABLES DEFINED

A campaign is made up of variables.

A common definition for *variable* is: "a quantity that may assume any one of a set of values" (*Merriam-Webster* Online).

That's fine, but let's give it a precise marketing definition: A variable is anything over which you have control that can change the outcome of a direct-response campaign.

In our nose ring campaign, a variable is your list—in this case, the people who read the publication you are using to distribute your flyers.

A storm that trashes your booth at the annual Nose Ring Fair is not a variable. You obviously can't control it, although it did affect your sales for the month.

The lead generation campaigns you will be studying are made up of variables, *things you can control.* By controlling all your variables, you can control your outcome. By controlling your outcome, you can control your commissions.

In this chapter I'm going to give you a quick overview of the *key* variables. When you understand them, you will understand the pieces that make up the campaigns we will be discussing. The first five variables I'm going to tell you about refer to the design or creation of the campaign. The last two refer to its execution.

A complete campaign is simply one in which you have thought through each variable. In subsequent chapters we will explore each of the variables in depth; here we will simply introduce them.

The list: I *always* begin developing a campaign by deciding first which list to use. It is probably impossible to state which variable has the most importance in the whole mix. However, in my opinion the list is by far the most important, but it probably receives the least amount of care and attention. I have run into both large and small companies that bought some commercially available lists without testing them. On the individual level, I have seen countless salespeople grab the first list they can find and start calling. Since they keep no records, they have no clue as to whether they have a good list or a bad list, or even what day it is, for that matter.

The list, as a variable, is too important to be treated in this manner. It's where good lead generation begins.

The campaign objective: I define *objective* as the degree of hotness intended for a response. You can design a campaign to find red cherries or green cherries. You can even design it to find hot prospects or even buyers. Campaigns for high-end products and services should be designed to attract red cherries or info leads. While there is a can of worms here, for now, just know that the objective of a lead generation campaign is always a lead, hotter or colder. You need the name of a person more or less ready to begin the development process.

The style: *Style* is defined as the medium or combination of media used to produce the response. Are you going to send a letter and follow it up with a phone call? Are you going to call first? Are you going to walk door-to-door? How are you going to achieve your campaign objective? When you make that decision, then you have decided upon the style.

The primary benefit: This is the main advantage someone will enjoy if they buy your product. It is normally embedded in the headline of an ad, letter, fax, email, or opening section of your telephone script or web page. It may be explicitly stated: "Cover up that bald spot." Or it can be implied: "Bald spot growing?"

The offer: The offer is something you propose to give the client in exchange for some time. "Free sample: bald spot scalp paint."

The headline in your ad or your opening benefit statement in your script is intended to generate enough interest to buy you the time to make your offer. The offer generates action. They have to respond to receive the offer.

The message: This is what you actually say in your calls, ads, and written messages. It comprises the words. It makes up your script. It is the copy for your letters. There are definite rules for constructing these vitally important pieces of your campaign. We'll go over these rules in a bit. Break them at your peril.

The sound: How you sound. Once you have developed your scripts and letters, it's time to fire up the campaign. If you are cold-calling, how you sound is vital. If you are taking incoming phone calls, how you sound says a tremendous amount about you.

If I had to pick one of these variables as second in importance to the list, I would choose sound, the way you sound on the telephone. I cannot tell you the number of times people have told me that a telephone-based campaign doesn't work, yet when I did it myself or gave it to someone with proven telephone skills, it worked quite well. The wild-card difference is how you sound.

The numbers: You have heard it said that sales is a numbers game. It is. Normally, when I am debugging a campaign, my first question is, "How many letters are you sending a week, a month?" Or, "How many calls are you making an hour?" If I hear five, or some other ridiculously low number, I *know* that I could have a highly successful campaign on my hands, but the players are not cranking enough numbers into it. The numbers of a campaign are the easiest thing to control.

THE SECOND MOST IMPORTANT QUESTION YOU'LL EVER ASK ABOUT PROSPECTING

Before getting to this, I want to remind you that we've already asked and answered the most important question: *How long does it take to find out if a person is a prospect?*

The answer: less than a minute.

With two or three quick questions, you can find out: Does this person have any interest? Can this person decide? Can this person afford your product?

Here's the second most important question: *How long does it take to find out if a particular campaign itself is a cherry or a pit?*

The answer: a lot less time than you think.

The subject we're introducing, then, is *campaign evaluation.* If you do not evaluate your campaign, you will be stuck at some point with a loser, and you might miss a winner, and you will be a hurtin' dog. Over its life, there is only one way to evaluate a campaign: profitability. Response rate, as long as it's greater than zero, doesn't necessarily matter if your campaign is profitable. I have run campaigns that produced an enormous response but failed miserably because the people responding were nonbuyers lured in by some free offer I made.

I've also run campaigns with a tiny response rate, even 0.25 percent or so, that was wildly profitable because a very high percentage of the respondents bought an expensive product. So, at a very minimum, you need to keep track of your expenses, your responses, your buyers, and the total revenue, and then calculate whether your campaign makes any money.

In the shorter run, though, don't be shy about making quick, even snap evaluations, and kicking your losers to the curb and look for better ones. Many loser campaigns can be spotted after a few hours or a few thousand mailings. But to verify a winner, you need to track it all the way through and find out what happened to the leads it generated. How many of them became good prospects, and of those, how many bought?

Understanding variables is vital when it comes to modifying a campaign. Here's the rule: If, early in the testing of a campaign, it does not seem to be working, change one variable. (If you change a whole bunch, you'll never know which of the changes were good . . . or bad.) Then back to testing. If your campaign starts to look good (we'll define "good" shortly), don't change anything; just keep prospecting. In the meantime, let the leads you're generating move through the pipeline. Keep good records so you can figure out if *enough* of the leads you're generating can be developed into hot prospects and turned over to your salespeople, who get them to buy your product or service and so make the campaign *profitable*. So suppose you send out a few thousand letters, get a couple of replies, and end up with no sales. What should you do? Remember the definition of *variable*? It's anything over which you have control. You can control response by changing a variable—perhaps your list. Run it again. This time you get ten responses and a couple of solid appointments that look good.

Perhaps it will take only one sale to guarantee success. If you get it, maybe this is a home run. If you don't get it, maybe you'd better generate ten more leads and see what happens. At some point in monitoring your results, you will conclude that you have either a winner or a loser.

If it's a winner, roll it out.

If it's a loser, change another variable. Or if you have changed several already, it's time to ditch this campaign and start all over.

All of which leads us to . . .

THE FOUR BASIC MISTAKES

Over the years I have seen far too many salespeople fail—many, if not most, needlessly. By paying very close attention to the four mistakes that follow, you can ensure that you don't follow them down the slippery slope.

1. Fail to keep adequate records so that campaigns can be evaluated

I guarantee that if you do not evaluate your campaigns, you will throw out lots of babies with their dirty bathwater. Or worse, you will toss the babies and keep the bathwater. If you do not keep records of your campaigns and periodically review those records, you will wind up, at the end of the month, quarter, year, or career, with far less than you should. You will have retained failing campaigns and thrown out winners.

2. Get a bad idea and stick to it

One of the reasons why rookie lead generators or salespeople go toes up is that they get a bad campaign and then stick to it. They are not failing because they fail to work hard. All too frequently, they work like Roman galley slaves. But what they're doing is just not effective. Sometimes, when confronted with numbers that demonstrate the campaign is failing, they still want to stick to the blasted thing. Why? Maybe it's the "winning isn't everything, it's the only thing" attitude. Maybe it worked for someone else. Maybe they don't want to fail. Throwing out a failing campaign is seen as failure rather than as common sense.

You need to understand that there's nothing wrong with failure in direct-response marketing. Expect failure more than success. You may need only one good campaign to ensure that you'll retire well-off if not downright rich. Perhaps you go through twenty or thirty or forty or even fifty campaigns to find the one that works for you. Are you a failure? No. Quite the opposite. You are smart by throwing out or changing something that doesn't work. Are you a success? Maybe not yet, but if you keep trying one campaign after another, you will be. Wildly so.

3. Get a good idea and change it

This is an insidious mistake. I've committed it many times myself and have tried to buffer my own tendency to do it by having people around me who have enough sense to say, "But, Bill, we did it differently last time and it worked great. Don't change it!"

One of my staff members was recently investigating why a particular direct-mail letter we had used successfully did not seem to be working.

As she went back through our records, she found that I had made some changes in an effort to improve it. When the changes didn't work, instead of reverting to the original letter, we decided that the campaign no longer worked. We then canceled the campaign. In doing so, we committed basic mistake number 3. When we dug out the original version of the campaign and reran it, it worked like a champ, just as it always had.

The big danger in basic mistake number 3, then, is assuming that a once-successful campaign doesn't work when you in fact have run an altered version of it.

4. Get a good idea and don't do it enough

There are lots of salespeople who had a good idea but didn't really roll it out. Perhaps you sent out a mailing and made a ton of money but then didn't do it for a while, if ever again. It's not uncommon to hear people say, "It worked so well I quit doing it." (Not my statement!) When you get the good profitable idea, go to the bank, mortgage your house, sell your second car, and cancel your kids' allowance. Roll it out. And stay with it.

SUMMARY

In this chapter you have learned:

What makes up a campaign;
How to modify a campaign to make it work;
How to modify a working campaign to make it *not* work—by changing
   one or more variables; and
Your ability to control your variables determines your success in direct
   marketing.

10

Campaign Development Checklist

Fish or cut bait.
—*Bill Good, age nine*

We had taken a family vacation to Cape Hatteras, North Carolina. My mother wanted "the boys"—me, my brother Ed, and my dad—to go fishing. She would stay in the cottage we had rented and read a book.

I ran the usual child guilt trip: "Mom, we don't get enough quality time. This should be a family fishing trip." Reluctantly, she concurred.

So we bought some mullet for bait. It was flapping around a little bit. I handed her my Boy Scout knife and said, "Cut us some bait."

She picked up a mullet and it flapped.

"Oh!" she screamed. "I can't! I didn't want to come on this! This is a boy thing!"

Calmly taking control of the deteriorating situation, I said, "Mother, you can fish." Turning to my little brother, "Ed, cut bait."

Someone must have misunderstood what I said, because by the time I was ten, poor Ed got left out of the statement altogether and it morphed simply into "Fish or cut bait." I believe it was used as a political slogan that year.

At any rate, this chapter, on the Campaign Development Checklist, is where you decide to become a fisherperson or a bait cutter. Follow campaign development procedure and you are a fisherperson. Don't do the hard work and fly by the seat of your pants and you are a los . . . er . . . bait cutter.

In this chapter we're going to introduce a key tool for developing campaigns, the Campaign Development Checklist.

Developing a campaign is a step-by-step process. You need to think it through in sequence and then do it in sequence. A substantial part of your success in designing campaigns depends more on thinking rather than on doing.

The Campaign Development Checklist guides you through this process. It also will guide me as I teach you what you need to know about each variable so you can produce prize-winning campaigns for your business.

I have put a copy of this checklist in the download section for this chapter. Every time you want to design a campaign, my recommendation is that you print out the checklist and go through it step-by-step. This checklist is so important that I am not going to let you have it unless you read this chapter. Buried somewhere in this chapter is the password to download this checklist.

PROSPECTING BOOK

This is a campaign-focused prospecting book. I hope that after reading it the concept of a campaign will come to dominate the way you think about finding and developing prospects. It should dictate the way you organize your files, your computer, and your daily activities. Campaigns are the key to *sustained* successful prospecting.

As we develop a campaign, you would do well not just to read but also to work through the steps on the Campaign Development Checklist so that at the end of the book you have a campaign you can try out. If the campaign you develop produces predictably profitable results, it can make you rich. Each chapter or two in this section will take up one of the variables from the checklist. As you follow along, you will learn how to use each variable in your own campaign.

It's up to you. If your campaign is a hit, you could be on your way to fame and fortune. If it produces predictably unprofitable results, it can drive you out of business unless you dump it quickly. But since you now know about the four basic mistakes, you will keep good records and evaluate as you go. You will be able to continue changing unsuccessful campaigns until you get it right, and then you'll lock it in.

Keep this in mind: to succeed in sales, *you must have one or more profitable campaigns*. I know people who earn seven figures who have only one campaign. It worked so well they just kept doing it . . . and doing it . . . and doing it.

A WORD ABOUT CHECKLISTS

At Bill Good Marketing, Inc., we use many checklists, and they serve two main functions:

1. By using a checklist, you will not forget an important piece of your plan. And if you do forget, you just add the piece to the next version of the checklist.
2. If a key person decides to be sick, another member of the team can step in and complete the job.

So you might want to download the text of the checklist from www.hotprospectsbook.com now and print it out. Look on the chapter 10 download page. The password to download this checklist is jet. (That's the name of my German shepherd, who will bite you if you give the password to anyone who hasn't bought the book.)

ASSIGNMENT

Using the secret password hidden in this chapter, download your copy of the Campaign Development Checklist, print it out, and then use it as you read the remainder of Book 2.

11

Lists

Campaign Starting Point

When life gives you lemons, make lemonade.
—Bill Good, age nine

When I was nine, I had a friend named Charles Liff. I always called him "Liff," not Charles. One day, we were trying to figure out how to make some money. Charles asked his mother to give him some lemons so we could sell lemonade. I told my mom, "Hey, Mom, Liff gave us lemons to make lemonade." A friend of hers, Mrs. Farr, was over at the house. She must have thought "Liff" was "Life." Another famous statement was born from a trivial comment. I was on a roll.

Very Important Note: The next two chapters deal with the principles of list development. Various resources, such as list brokers, websites, and even some public library references, are posted on our "List Resources" page, which you can access through the downloads section for this chapter. The password is, naturally, buried deep in the chapter.

Neither of these chapters may be right for you. You may work for a large corporation that assigns you a number of accounts or even just one single account. You may work for or own a company that caters to a particular type of buyer in a given area, in which case your list is probably all the companies of that certain type. If this is the case, skip this chapter because your list, for better or for worse, has already been developed.

As you begin working your way through the Campaign Development Checklist, you hit the first and probably most important step: buy a list or develop one on your own.

While developing or buying a list seems like a one-time thing, it's not. If done correctly, it never ends. You get a good list. After a while, it's not so good anymore. You improve it. That's great. But then, after a while, it's not as good. You have to improve it or dump it.

The three steps of list development are:

1. Develop (or buy) a list of people you believe are likely prospects.
2. Improve your list by adding the names of people who are (a) like those now responding, and (b) if possible, who know each other so that word of mouth can occur.
3. If the campaign is a winner, continue to improve the list, which can sometimes go on for years.

Develop. Improve. Improve again. These are the three ongoing steps.

This chapter will cover how to find sources of names, develop those leads, and refine them. The next chapter will talk briefly about some small lists that can help improve your list in big ways.

THE IMPORTANCE OF LIST DEVELOPMENT

Your lists are to you what a claim is to a gold prospector. It's your spot by the river where you will either strike gold or not, succeed or not. Yet most salespeople don't spend even 1 percent of their time developing their lists. Too bad. To put a number to it, your list is at least 40 percent of your success in direct-response marketing.

Regrettably, too many salespeople are not willing to do the kind of work necessary to develop good lists. This brings to mind the classic story of two brothers who went up to their room and found it filled with horse manure. Needless to say, they were stunned. One burst into tears. But the other thought for a moment, smiled, and started digging like mad. The crybaby exclaimed, "What's wrong with you? Why are you digging?" The other brother said, "With all this crap, there's got to be a pony here somewhere."

The process of list development can, from one point of view, be compared to digging through a pile of manure looking for a pony. The work may be pungent and it's certainly no fun, but there is a pony in there. If you do the work, you'll find it.

THE PURPOSE OF LIST DEVELOPMENT

Every once in a while I have run into an old bit of accepted sales wisdom, undoubtedly held over from the Old Way, which emphatically states, "It doesn't matter who you call, but how many you call."

This is false. Not only does it matter who you mail to or call, but who you mail to or call can make a tremendous—indeed, unbelievable—difference in your overall results.

Sometimes you'll be surprised. A client of mine reported great success in cold-calling a list of new business licensees. He commented, "This list is so full of wannabes that no one ever calls it. But buried on it are a few very successful people starting their second or third business. That's where I'm striking pay dirt." (Mine.)

In prospecting, creative list development serves a very important function. It concentrates your cherries by putting more of them onto a single list, so you don't have to make as many calls or send as many letters to find a good prospect. Or, looking at it another way, it helps you screen out the pits in advance. If the telephone is part of your lead generation activities, and if you really hate picking up the phone, spend more time on developing your list. You'll spend less time later making those dreaded phone calls! And maybe if you're lucky, you might even start to like those calls, since they now generate a lot more money for you.

THE BASIC LAWS OF LISTS

After the first few years of the California gold rush, the "easy" claims were taken. It's the same with lists. In any highly competitive field, the easy lists have been clobbered by every new generation of salespeople that comes along. There is a point, after all, where repetition escalates into harassment, and someone receiving several calls a day has long since passed that point of being friendly. Attorneys, doctors, and other obvious categories from the Yellow Pages are cases in point.

This brings us to the two basic laws of lists:

1. The easier a list is to get, the more salespeople have it, and the less likely it is to be any good.
2. The harder a list is to get, the fewer salespeople have it, and the more profitable it's likely to be.

These laws explain why some salespeople *always* find more prospects than others. They have put in the time and the imagination to get better lists.

This I can tell you for sure: Your best lists will be developed through effort and creative thought. They won't be given to you by your sales manager, nor will you be able to buy them. This is not to say that buying lists is not important. It can be, depending on your market. But the very best ones are those you develop yourself.

WHAT IS A GOOD LIST?

Let's define a good list (named after me, of course) as follows:

A good list is any list of names, addresses, and phone numbers that has been put together based on one or more characteristics those people have in common. A good list produces better results than names taken from any major free source of information, such as the Yellow Pages.

To evaluate goodness, you need to be able to compare it with something else. To justify the time and the expense of developing a list, we need to know that your developed list is better than a list that is available for free.

Let me give you an example of "one or more characteristics those people have in common." If you define a list according to "occupation," the individuals have one characteristic in common, so we could get a list of lawyers. When we specify "lawyers in New York City" we have added a second characteristic in common. Suppose we say "female lawyers in New York City under age thirty-five." We now have four characteristics in common.

This is a list that one financial adviser used. She was a former attorney who understood attorneys, and she built up a fantastic clientele dealing only with people like herself, whom she understood, liked, and could relate to. As you develop your concept of a good list, you also may want to include the characteristic "someone I could like."

The more characteristics these potential prospects on your list have in common, the more likely you are to develop a presentation that will communicate to a relatively large percentage of them. This in turn produces more prospects per hour if you are calling rather than mailing to your list.

Go back to the definition of a good list again. Note the phrases "one or more characteristics those people have in common" and "major free source of information."

Let's take the flip side of the female attorney list. Let's say that you think attorneys are a lower life form, along the order of amoeba. To you, spending time with an attorney is like a field trip to a sewage plant. You would then, of course, take great care to exclude attorneys from your list. What's the point in coming to work in the morning if you are going to have to deal with people you don't like? I can't tell you how many salespeople I know who live half their lives in fear that some jerk they regrettably sold something to will call them up. Why even sell to them in the first place? If there are certain types of people you don't like, try your best to exclude them from your list. Failing that, don't sell to them.

If it's not fun, don't do it!

HOW GOOD IS "GOOD"?

The definition of a good list that we have been covering so far doesn't give you any idea of how good is good. So let's expand our definition.

A guaranteed good list is any list that will generate a minimum of one to two red cherries an hour when called or at least 8 percent when mailed. This is only a rule of thumb.

But your figures may be different, so let's pose an alternate definition: a good list is any list that generates a profitable response.

Until you know differently, use one to two red cherries an hour as your benchmark for goodness or an 8 percent mail response. Naturally, if you are getting less than that, the problem could be any of the other variables, but as you go through the testing process, changing these one at a time, you will conclude that you either can or cannot hit minimum targets. Once you determine you have a bad list, it's gone. Time to start over.

There is no question that some lists can be considered good at two red cherries an hour, one an hour, or even one every several hours. The exceptions to the one- or two-an-hour rule will depend in part on the price of the goods or service you're selling and the resistance level of your market.

If you are selling an office building worth $40 million, you would have to have an extraordinarily good list to get one or two people per hour interested in it. However, by researching real estate buyers for major insurance companies, private syndicates, and major public partnerships, you might well be able to come up with one every few hours.

If you are an insurance agent looking for pension-fund money, one red cherry every couple of hours might be the best you can do. This is an extremely competitive market, and some pension-fund managers get literally dozens of calls a day from insurance agents, consultants, and advisers.

If you can't conceivably come up with one to two red cherries per hour, then for you, a good list would be defined according to however many red cherries you, or the best prospector in your firm, can produce per hour given your best efforts.

I also should add that I am assuming forty to sixty dials per hour. If you're doing twelve calls an hour and not averaging even a red cherry an hour, don't blame me. Push up your numbers and then see what you can get (See "How to Make More Calls." It's in the bonus chapters section of our website. All you need is your personal password.)

LIST SELECTION PRINCIPLES

In the balance of this chapter, I'll go over two of the three principles of list development we'll be using. Since there are so many applications for sales prospecting, it would be impossible to give detailed sources for each industry. So my primary objective here and in the following chapter is to teach you to "think lists."

Once you know how to think about the subject and know your resources, you can:

- simply take a trip to the local public library, tell the librarian what you're looking for, and start;
- call your favorite list broker and find out what is available;
- log on to the Internet and mine the incredible resources there.

Soon you will be on your way to developing likely names.

DEVELOP YOUR CORE LIST

It's time for your first assignment: develop or buy a list of likely prospects.

How many names do you need? A few hundred to a few thousand would be an adequate start. At the end of this chapter, when you know more about list development, you can answer this question in greater detail.

We're going to use a single principle, the "look-alike principle," to develop your first list. (Of course, it's based on my famous statement "Birds of a feather flock together.") Then we'll use the look-alike principle again as well as the word-of-mouth principle to improve your lists.

Likely prospects: Your best prospect has characteristics similar to someone who has already bought your product or service, so we're looking for more people who resemble your clients. Obviously I don't mean resemble physically. I mean resemble demographically. (Demographics are the study of population characteristics such as gender, income, and occupation, especially as these characteristics may affect buying decisions.) Where do we get such a list? Here are some suggestions:

Likely Prospects: Residential Market

1. Same neighborhood or street as your current clients. On our "List Resources" page, we will show you current technology on how to create a map of where your current clients live. Remember, all you need is your personal password.
2. Same club, organization, or activity. Best bet here is just to ask. I know a financial adviser who joined a local Mercedes-Benz club. As he became known, it was easy to shift discussion from one high-value product to an investment.
3. Same age, income, race, and gender. Best sources: list brokers. I will cover them in detail.

    While the best lists are likely to be those you develop yourself, don't mess around if you are just getting started. Make a quick call to your friendly list broker. Get started. Improve as you go.

Likely Prospects: Business Market

1. Same building. The resources available to find this type of info keep changing. So frequently check our "List Resources" page.
2. Same SIC (Standard Industrial Classification) code—a numerical coding system developed by the U.S. Department of Commerce to classify similar businesses. If you work in the business market-

place, I have a real treat for you on how to develop prospects just like the clients you already have. The best source is covered thoroughly on the "List Resources" page.

3. Same occupation (purchasing agent, human resources director). Best sources: list brokers.

4. Same-size business. Best sources: list brokers.

Online Mapping for Residential or Business Prospect Lists

As I write this, there has been an explosion in the use of satellite imagery on the web. It has profound implications to certain businesses. You will find current recommendations for mapping services on the "List Resources" page.

Suppose you sell swimming pools. With the latest from Google, Microsoft, or others, you can zoom in close enough to tell who does and who does not have a pool.

Or you sell roofing. You can even measure the sizes of the roofs of various commercial buildings, and in some cases you can tell whether they need a "free inspection." Why spend hours calling when you can spend far less time calling people you already *know* need your service?

WHAT'S NEXT?

That wasn't hard, was it?

Once you have developed or purchased your core list, you will continue developing the rest of the campaign. When you have all the pieces put together, you will test the campaign. You will try your direct-mail piece on the list, or you will call it. If you hit in at two or three red cherries per hour or pull at least 0.8 percent, you probably have a campaign you can take to the bank. If not, you need to change your script or direct-mail letter, the number of calls you're making, and so on, and try to get the number into the "good" range. If you can't, you need to go back to square one (mine) and come up with a new core list. If you can get a list in range, it's time to start improving it.

ASSIGNMENT

Complete the "develop core list" step on the Campaign Development Checklist.

12

Improve Your Core Lists

Naturally, you want to develop your own campaign "by the book." I was eleven when I came up with the "by the book" statement. My brother and I were constructing a giant building with our Erector sets. He wanted to get creative. I said, "Ed, let's do it by the book." A friend of my dad's ran a little publishing company, long since out of business, and he made this his advertising slogan.

Once you have some lists that produce acceptable results, the name of the game is to improve them. You do this by adding names that, hopefully, are better. To add these names, you really have to know your clients and good prospects.

In short, to make these list improvements, you need to learn to think like a fisherperson. Suppose you are going fishing in the morning, but your alarm doesn't go off, and you get a late start. As you walk down to the lake, you see an old codger with a string of fish thrown over his shoulder. Naturally, you have some questions.

YOU: Where did you catch 'em?
CODGER: Down at the lake.

Now, if you are not much of a fisherperson, you would let it go at that and wander on down to the lake. But if you are a real fisherperson, you would continue the conversation.

YOU: Where down at the lake?
CODGER: By the big rock.
YOU: You mean the one over by the willow trees?

CODGER: Yep.
YOU: What were you using for bait?
CODGER: Plastic worm.
YOU: Great. Thanks.

Look at your present clients as if they were that string of fish hanging from the codger's back. What pond did they come from? Or to put it in sales prospecting terms, what list could they have come from?

You are looking for the lists of people where your client's name would be. You are looking for the same characteristics in a prospect that your current clients already share. Ideally, the people on the list will have some connection that will make word of mouth possible. Given a choice between a list of people who own a Mercedes-Benz and a Mercedes-Benz owners' club directory, always take the list on which word of mouth can occur—in this case, the owners' club directory.

LIST IMPROVEMENT PRINCIPLES

To improve your core lists, you will use two principles:

1. You have already met one of these: the look-alike principle. We used this to develop the initial batch of names. Now we're going to use it to improve the list by defining the characteristics even more precisely so they match those characteristics belonging to your current clients. For example: You sell computer equipment and get a big order from a medical practice. Now you put on your fisherperson's hat and start asking questions: What kind of practice is this? Does the type of practice—say, laser eye surgery—have anything to do with them ordering a new computer system? If the answer is yes—because, as a business, laser eye surgery is growing like weeds after a rainstorm—then obviously you don't want to focus just on doctors' offices but also on medical practices performing laser eye surgery.

   How would you find them? I would look up this type of practice by using one of the resources in the "List Resources" of our website. I would then find out what its SIC code is, and subsequently pull all those SIC codes in my market area. I might get only a few names, but they still would be added to my list. That's just how I would do it, and have done it, and it's worked for me.

2. The second of these principles is the word-of-mouth principle. If at all possible, find a list on which word of mouth can occur. This is so

important that if I could yell at you right now to get the point across, I would. It's what I did in selling seminars to various financial services and insurance firms. Going way back to the beginning of my business, I cracked E. F. Hutton and Farmers Insurance by simply asking the one contact I had in each firm if I could have the list of branch managers. These were the best prospect lists I ever developed. They held the same job and knew each other. It was easy to spread the word because they all went to the same meetings and shared war stories.

Here are some possibilities that may combine tightly defined look-alike lists with lists of people who know each other. (The best way to get these lists is by asking. Don't be shy; most people are genuinely happy to help. The others, well, we know their classification, don't we?)

IMPROVED PROSPECT LISTS: BUSINESS

Best practices lists: Major corporations have meetings with other companies they don't directly compete with to share best practices. Can you get that list? You can at least ask, can't you?

Trade associations: Chances are that your good corporate clients belong to several trade associations. Ask which ones your client belongs to. If you feel comfortable doing so, ask for the list. Otherwise, call the association and ask how you can buy it. Check the home page of the association.

Same occupation: Suppose your best client is the chief legal counsel of a publicly traded company. Naturally, you want a list of chief legal counsels. There might be an association, which you could find out about by asking your client. Or you might check the home pages of similar publicly traded companies. Worst-case scenario: you have to call all the companies and ask the receptionist for the name of the chief legal counsel.

IMPROVED PROSPECT LISTS: RESIDENTIAL

Same condo development: There are lots of ways to get this type of list, all of which are covered on our "List Resources" page. When developing this type of list, make sure you get the unit number of each condo, especially if you are doing a mail campaign. The U.S. Postal Service will not always deliver letters to an apartment or condo development unless you specify which apartment or condo number.

Same hobby: As you learn more about your clients, ask them how they spend their spare time. You may find that they do everything from collecting stamps to playing ball to participating in square dance clubs. Ask for those lists. If you can't get them that way, call the club president and offer to join as an associate member. Many of these groups can be joined for $10 to $25, and you get the membership directory when you join. There are countless lists you can obtain, filled with people just like your best clients, and on which word of mouth can then occur. As you develop these lists, you can be sure that your response rate to your mailing and phoning campaigns will improve.

PUBLIC RECORD INFORMATION

Since I don't know what company you work for and what kind of list you need to develop, I can't be certain I've given you any good ideas so far. So in the next few pages I'm going to come at the problem from a different perspective. Instead of trying to help you identify lists of people who look just like your current clients, I'm going to give you some resources I have used in various campaigns. As you look these over, you may be struck by the fact that your client appears on one or more of these lists.

There is an absolute wealth of information available for free in public records and libraries. But since the information requires some digging, it constitutes a different kind of "free" than what you would find in the Yellow Pages. The free information you can find here can make up some pretty good lists. Don't complain about bad lists if you haven't spent a few hours following the trails I'm outlining here.

On our "List Resources" page we will give you current information on how to find names in these categories.

Licenses or permits: The best way to find out if public records are restricted in your state, such as being required by the state to operate a license, is to call a list broker. If the records are available, your local list broker will have them. Does one of your clients own a factory that disposes of toxic waste? I guarantee they have to have some kind of permit. The names of permit holders are available through a list broker or through the city, county, or state licensing agency.

Property tax records: In the United States and Canada, and possibly other countries whose legal system descended from England's common-law system, property tax records are open to public inspection and copying. The theory seems to be that to ensure that property is assessed fairly, we as citizens should be able to see what our neighbor is paying for his or her property. Among other things, you can tell when the property was purchased, its assessed valuation, how it's titled, and how it's zoned.

Property tax records typically do not contain phone numbers. These records are available in several forms. In major metro areas they are available online or at the county property tax assessor's office. In smaller communities they may still be on microfiche. Best bet: visit your local assessor's office, ask someone how the records are kept, and have him or her explain them to you.

LIBRARY RESOURCES

There is one key to unlocking the vast resources of a library: the librarian. Library resources change. But as long as there are books, there will be librarians.

And guess what? Many librarians are becoming information search consultants. They can help you find what you want both in the library and online, and not always with a simple Google search.

Over the years, as I have researched different lists for different marketing campaigns, I have come to learn that if you take some time at the business desk of your local library, you may discover your very best resource. Remember, these folks answer questions all day long about library, and now Internet, resources. If I were to give you an assignment to "learn all local resources for developing good lists," I would put at the very top of this instruction: "Find out which librarian in your biggest library knows the most about directories, local publications, and Internet access. Befriend this person."

Let's take a couple of examples: I asked a financial adviser client who his best client was. He said, "It's a guy who designs packaging for different products."

"Would you like to have more like him?" I asked.

His reply was "Are you kidding? I've checked the Yellow Pages and there are none listed." He was certainly correct that package designers were not listed in the Yellow Pages. They tend to work for big corporations and advertising agencies, and so are not listed separately.

To get a list of package designers, we asked a librarian who helped us find a trade association for package designers based in New York with some three thousand members. The adviser called them and asked, "How many members do you have in Southern California?"

"Four hundred."

He then asked, "How do I get a copy of the membership directory?"

"Send me twenty-seven dollars" was the reply.

Now how many advisers do you think regularly prospect the list of package designers? Not many. And that's the entire idea.

Suppose you sell a software product to human resources departments. Instead of cold-calling companies trying to find out who the manager of that department is, find out which trade association they belong to and see if you can join as an associate member. It's easier than you think. Marian the business librarian is your best resource.

LIST BROKERAGE RESOURCES

There are thousands of companies that sell lists of various kinds. In most cases, list brokers are truly brokers, meaning that they broker a product they don't own. For example, a broker may sell a list of magazine subscribers. The magazine owns the list, not the broker, who just receives a commission for selling it. Depending on your needs, a list broker may be vital in your efforts to build good or even great prospecting lists.

List brokers have access to a website created by a company named Standard Rate and Data. It's a database of thousands of lists. If there is a list of one-armed window washers in New Jersey, a list broker can find it on this website. You can, too—if you want to pay a bucket of money to subscribe. Best bet: use a list broker.

When you call a list broker, you need to know as much as possible about the kind of names you want. If you are prospecting people at their homes, you want to know their age range, income range, location, whether they rent or own their home, if they have children, what kind of cars they drive, and so on. The more information you can give a list broker, the better job he or she can do in locating the ultimate look-alike list for you.

Let the list broker do his or her job.

You will find our current recommended list brokers on the "List Resources" page on our website. You just need your personal password.

HOW MANY NAMES DO YOU NEED?

This is a tough question, and the answer varies tremendously by industry and quality of list. You don't need an infinite number of names. When you get a good list, you'll keep it and contact the people again and again by mail or phone in forty-five- to ninety-day intervals, depending on your industry and product. How many do you need? There are a few rules of thumb for contacting your list.

1. If you are prospecting a residential market, you will need about eight thousand names, if you are new in the business. Unless you want to call the few superprocrastinators who never got around to registering for the "Do Not Call" registry, you'll be mailing to your list of names. Eight thousand names will generate five hundred letters a week, more or less, for about three months, with some left over as you take names off the list.

2. In the business-to-business marketplace, you'll need to do some arithmetic to figure out how many names you need. First, figure out how many contacts it takes for you to achieve your weekly objective. Let's say you are a commercial leasing agent and that you want to see ten new people each week. To set up one appointment you need to contact twenty people on your look-alike list. So to set up ten appointments, you need to contact two hundred (ten times twenty) people each week. That's a lot of cold-calling. The good news is, as you begin following up and calling the red and green cherries you have generated in previous weeks, the number of calls you have to make each week will come way down.

   Now, multiply your weekly needs by eight. So in this case, you will need sixteen hundred names (eight times two hundred). This gives you enough names to last eight weeks. Then, if you are getting your ten people in the shop each week, and if your list is profitable to you, start back at the beginning and recontact your prospects.

ASSIGNMENT

Go to your nearest big public library. Find a librarian in the business section. Tell him or her some of the characteristics of the kind of person you would like to find. Learn library resources.

13

Small Lists

Small is beautiful.
—Bill Good, age nine

When I was nine, I took art lessons and became fascinated with miniature drawing. One day I made a tiny drawing. It was so small you had to have a magnifying glass to see that it was not just a dot on the page. My mother said, "Don't you think bigger would be better?" I smiled and said, "Mom, small is beautiful." Later, some economist picked this up out of the atmosphere and wrote a series of books called *Small Is Beautiful*, never once, of course, giving me credit.

It is appropriate for a chapter on small lists to also be short. So here goes.

If you truly hate to cold-call and mail, and if you are in any kind of corporate services, consulting, financial services, commercial real estate, or computer software or hardware business, you should pay very close attention to this short chapter.

You need to build lists of companies in the process of change. You're really looking for money in motion.

Companies or people in the process of change find additional change easier to make.

You can use change lists for two purposes: (1) to replace names you have removed from your core lists, or (2) as your primary list, especially if you can get enough of these names to develop your target number of new clients.

Because it's hard to get these names, the lists will be small. But they can and probably will be your very best lists. According to me, "Small is beautiful."

You will find our up-to-date change list resources on the "List Resources" page.

14

The Campaign Objective

I am going to assume in this chapter that you are a manager. Even if you are a rookie, you may have to cover the entire spectrum, from lead generation to lead development to sales, and (gasp) even service. If you cover these functions, then you are a sales manager, whether you like it or not.

The term *campaign objective* refers to the hotness we intend a lead to have when it is first generated.

Do you want people to set appointments when they respond? Or are you okay if they request information that is then sent out?

I am fully aware that many readers of this book are stuck, for the time being, doing their own lead generation and lead development. You may also be doing your own data entry, hardly an activity I would have someone worth $1,000 an hour doing.

According to me, we have to start somewhere. We are going to start this section by separating the lead generation, lead development, computer operations, and sales functions. For now these may all be lodged in the same person but hopefully not for long.

Let's get back to the subject of the campaign objective.

As a lead generator and lead developer, how much do you want your salesperson (who may also be you) to deal with cold or lukewarm leads? Deciding which type of lead you want is the first step in defining the campaign objective. Let's look at some possible objectives and some things you'll need to think about in choosing one.

POSSIBLE CAMPAIGN OBJECTIVES

The problem with hot prospects is that there are not enough of them.

Remember, a hot prospect is someone very interested, financially qualified, and willing to begin the sales process. When a prospect says "I want to see you," that's a hot prospect. Someone who will set up a telephone appointment is hot. But people who request information first . . . well, they are not as hot. So once again, here's our "lead hotness thermometer" in operation.

Four gradations on the lead thermometer refer to campaign objectives. So let's look at them more closely this time from the point of view of deciding what we want a campaign to produce.

A: HOT PROSPECT

A hot prospect is as good as it gets in terms of a lead, but you do not frequently generate these on a first response.

You would almost always have to use Old Way methods to strong-arm your way into someone's office or home.

I'm not going to say you cannot use "hot prospect" as your campaign objective, because the minute I say, "no way," someone will say, "but I did it."

Nevertheless, you would have to have an extraordinary offer and an incredible list.

Rule of thumb: Don't start here. Cultivate cooler leads instead. Work them up to hot through lead development. Asking too much too soon can blow a lead right out of your pipeline.

B: RED CHERRY

A red cherry lead in this context would be someone who has responded, is presumably qualified for decision-making capability, and has funds available now.

Red cherries normally are generated on a telephone-based campaign. We don't know if someone responding to a direct-mail campaign is qualified, so they are generally classified as a D, info lead.

C: GREEN CHERRY

Designing a campaign to generate primarily green cherries is interesting. While I have not done it much, I have done it enough to know that it can be very successful. Such a campaign would take virtually all the pressure off someone. "I realize you are not interested now, but I wonder if I could ask you a couple of questions to see if this is something you might consider down the road."

D: INFO LEAD

For any kind of direct-mail or email campaign, I usually go for an info lead. This is the classic direct-mail-style campaign where people request a free report, free booklet, or whatever other material you have available.

You have to pay a lot of attention to how the response arrives in your office.

With the exception of trade-show leads, which are probably even a bit cooler than info leads, the response will typically arrive on one of four channels:

1. Call in
2. Fax in a reply
3. Mail in a reply
4. Register on website

Once I did a thorough study of people responding to my direct mail. I found that almost all of the people who bought our service called in. A much lower percentage of people who became clients sent in a coupon or faxed a reply. So I cut out the other response options.

But things have changed. Now many of our direct-mail campaigns are designed to drive people to the web. Tracking where our sales come from showed a decided shift in the way in which people responded. As a result, some of our lead generation campaigns are only intended to get people to our website.

Once we have generated the lead with direct mail, our lead developers then call, provide additional information, verify that price is not a problem at this time, and then go to work to move them up the thermometer.

When the prospect starts asking very specific questions, has been qualified and requalified for money, and appears very interested, a telephone appointment will be set with one of my salespeople. But I get ahead of myself.

CAMPAIGNS FOR ROOKIES: WILLING TO TALK

When breaking in rookie lead developers, you have to realize they don't know much and can mess up a lead that probably cost a lot of money to generate, so we recommend a mail/phone campaign. The campaign objective is to find a potential prospect who is not necessarily qualified for money but just willing to talk. In this case, the salesperson would act as the lead developer.

In this type of campaign, a letter is mailed and followed with a phone call a few days after receipt.

When your rookie caller gets the prospect to the phone, he or she simply says, "This is Joe Blow's office calling with Reliable Widget. Mr. Blow sent you some information about our new oscillating widget. Would you like to speak with him about it?"

If so, the prospector turns the lead over to a salesperson or sets a time within the next few minutes that the person would receive a phone call from the salesperson.

As your rookies learn more about your company, product, or service, you turn over more and more of the lead development process to them until they can warm a prospect from lukewarm to hot.

These are our objectives. How do we pick one?

HOW TO PICK AN OBJECTIVE

There is no hard-and-fast rule in picking a campaign objective. It's not a mechanical process. But there are some things you might consider.

1. Consider your resources

If your salespeople have no support, obviously they are responsible for both phases of prospecting, so the highest objective your campaign could go would be a red cherry lead. If you have a very small mailing list, you can't afford to miss a single opportunity. If this is the case, you might want to invest a lot of resources to get your best salesperson talking to one of these prospects.

2. Strength of your offer

Let's assume your offer is a 50 percent price decrease on a well-known product for a limited time. You could have your lead generators jump on the phone, do a blitz, and set up prequalified appointments. But if your offer is the same thing they've heard for years, you will have to sell it harder, which means you may have to settle for finding a prospect who is interested in talking.

3. How well-known is your firm?

If you are the lead dog in the pack, it may be very easy to make appointments. If nobody has ever heard of you, you may have to drop down a couple of notches in prospect temperature and perhaps only look for someone willing to talk.

4. Resistance level of the market

If lots of similar companies are pounding the same marketplace, put lots of support behind your best salesperson so that when contact is made, you can "put your best foot forward" (to quote myself, of course).

5. Skill level of your callers

If you have lead developers whose job is to set up appointments for your salespeople, then the more skilled they are, the more able they will be to warm up those prospects, develop red cherries, and perhaps even hot prospects. But if they are just starting out, their first assignment might well be simply to connect people to the salesperson without any or with very little explanation.

6. Value of your salesperson's time

A huge impact on a salesperson's and a company's bottom line can be produced by shifting the objective up or down in terms of temperature. If you have a star salesperson, my inclination would be to surround that person with the best support staff you have available. The more time that star is in front of your clients and prospects, the more revenue will be generated.

ASSIGNMENT

Your assignment is to take the checklist you printed when you read chapter 10, "Campaign Development Checklist," and decide on an objective for the campaign you will create as you work through this book.

15

How to Pick a Style

You can read the writing on the wall.
—Bill Good, age ten

In the fourth grade, a close friend, who sat just behind me in class, dipped his finger in the finger paint, wrote some stupid expression on the wall, and signed my name to it. He expected I would "take the fall" (also mine). When accused, I pointed to him and told the teacher, "Read the writing on the wall for yourself. Do you really think I would write something that stupid?" I think she must have mentioned my statement to someone in the teachers' lounge. It was famous within months.

Let's review for just a moment. A variable is anything over which you have control that can change the outcome of a campaign. Campaign style is a variable. Changing the style—the medium or combination of media used to produce the campaign objective—will normally have a huge impact on the outcome because so much is affected when you change it.

Campaign styles are named according to the medium or series of media used to generate the result.

Mail/phone is a style requiring a letter followed by a phone call. You also could have an email/phone or a fax/phone campaign.

You will find a summary list of styles in the Campaign Development Checklist.

When you come to this step on the checklist you probably already have an idea of what kind of campaign you want to employ, and it certainly won't take more than a few seconds to execute this step. It will take far longer for you to read this chapter and understand campaign styles than it will to pick the style according to the guidelines laid down here.

The style of your campaign determines the sequence of promotional actions you will take to execute your campaign. The style also defines its parts. So let's give some thought to this step.

In picking a style, you want a campaign that will achieve the objective with the least amount of time, effort, and expense while still conforming to how you like to run your sales business.

Just as there is no rote way to choose the campaign objective, there is no rote way to pick a style.

If you hate direct mail and think it doesn't work, don't use it. If you don't want anyone working for you and want to do it all yourself, you probably would choose a phone/mail/phone style. If you work a residential market (home improvement, investments, insurance, real estate), you need to figure out a way to first get permission to call. Trade shows, walking door-to-door, and mailings that drive people to Internet sites are all options.

So with your campaign objective in mind, look over the list of styles and pick the one that is most consistent with your objective. To put it another way, pick a style and try it. If it doesn't work, try a different one.

To quote myself: "There is more than one way to skin a cat."

Very Important Note: No matter which campaign style you select, the prospects you generate will fall into one or more of our prospect types: hot, red, green, info lead. These types are then developed with the standard set of lead development scripts and messages. These are covered in chapters 23, "Lead Development Scripts," and chapter 24, "Lead Development Messages."

CAMPAIGN STYLES EXPANDED

Let's take a moment to define each style and list the promotional elements involved in running the different styles of campaign. These are the scripts, letters, and other pieces you will need.

Unless otherwise stated, the messages will be found in the lead development messages you can download as part of your chapter 24, "Lead Development Messages," assignment. The scripts can be found in the download section for chapter 23, "Lead Development Scripts."

Phone/Mail/Phone

1. Call and offer people information on a topic you believe the prospects on your list will find of interest. When you discover the interest, you then qualify for money, decision capability, and time.
2. Send requested information.
3. Follow up according to lead type. Use the procedures in your "Prospect Action Cheat Sheet."

Campaign Objective

Red cherry.

Required Elements

1. Phone/mail/phone first-call script
2. Phone/mail/phone second-call script
3. Information to send out
4. Lead development messages:* red cherry or red cherry–email

Background

This is the first campaign style I developed. I got the idea for it when I was teaching rookies at E. F. Hutton how to cold-call. Instead of trying to open an account on the first call, which was the then accepted method, I separated the call into a prospecting call and a selling call and created a multicall system. Tens of thousands, even hundreds of thousands of salespeople who have attended my seminars and read my earlier books have implemented this style campaign.

---

* These are names of messages. When you see "email" as part of a message name, it just means it's the same message but formatted for email. Same words, different channel. See the download page for chapter 20.

Comment

If you're not sure which style to use, choose this style. In a very few calls, you can get a good idea of how resistant or responsive your marketplace is. The start-up costs for this style of campaign are close to nothing. In addition, it's very easy to revise without having to change a whole bunch of printed material or other expensive items. Very possibly you should consider this campaign style as the campaign before the campaign. It's your survey, your testing ground.

Mail/Phone

In this style, you send a letter (or fax or email) and follow it three to five days later with a phone call.

Campaign Objective

A hot prospect. But we'll also accept red cherries and info leads. This is the only cold-prospecting campaign I have designed that can produce hot prospects on a first call. It's always worth a try to see if you can profitably produce hot prospects. If it works, you have shortened your sales pipeline. If it doesn't—oh well. Go after red cherries instead.

Required Elements*

1. Preapproach letter using one of the message formats (see chapter 20, "Lead Generation Letters: How to Have Good Letters Even if You're Not a Good Letter Writer")
2. Business-reply envelope
3. Mail/phone follow-up script—rookie version, or mail/phone follow-up script—established lead generator version
4. Mail/phone first-call options

Background

This campaign was developed primarily for business owners and corporate executives who are notoriously difficult to reach by phone. By

---

* Scripts mentioned in this chapter are thoroughly covered in chapter 19. Just wait until you get there.

sending the letter, sometimes addressed to the assistant, you can then legitimately say you are following up on your correspondence.

Comment

What makes this work is the headline (or subject line, if email) of the message, because it ties the follow-up script to the message. For example,
    Headline of message: BALD SPOT GROWING?
    Follow-up script: Good morning, Mr. Hairless. We sent you an email this morning headlined "Bald spot growing?" Does that ring a bell?

Message

In a message campaign, instead of asking to speak to the decision-maker, you get the name of his or her screener and leave a message. Try to avoid being sent to voice mail. By getting someone else to write down what you say, you are in essence delivering more than thirty handwritten messages an hour. No postage. No paper.

Campaign Objective

A hot prospect or a red cherry.

Required Elements

1. A short message, less than fifty words
2. Incoming-call script

Background

As I recall, this campaign style grew out of an attempt to reach people who cannot be reached in any other way. Just try getting through to a doctor or a dentist. It's like calling nowhere. But if you can leave enough messages, and if the prospect, sequestered behind multiple layers of defense screen, is desirable enough, a few return calls can more than justify the effort.

Comment

The message can offer a free seminar, free report, or whatever. Basically, you are running a telephone-based campaign almost like a direct-mail campaign, except in this case you are delivering handwritten messages instead of letters. At a minimum, go for thirty dials per hour. After a few hours, shut it off and see if anyone calls.

I know of one financial adviser who built a very large business by hiring several callers who would only call and leave messages with doctors.

Standard Direct Mail

In a standard direct-mail campaign, you send out letters with some form of information request, coupon, or reply card. If it's a good letter sent to a good list, a profitable number of people will respond by calling or sending in the response card.

When the response comes in, send out what was promised.

The promised materials can be as simple as a white paper or as fancy as a brochure or a DVD.

Seven days later, follow up the information request with a phone call.

Campaign Objective

Info lead.

All we know when someone replies is that they are interested. On the follow-up call, find out what kind of lead (or no lead) you have.

Required Elements

1. Standard direct-mail letter format
2. Business-reply envelope
3. Information to be sent out as requested
4. Direct-mail follow-up script
5. Incoming-call qualification script

Background

Having written for *Barron's Business* and *Financial Weekly* as well as numerous newspapers and magazines, the transition to direct mail was relatively easy for me. In about 1980, I discovered the bible for anyone in the field of direct-response advertising: *Tested Advertising Methods* by John Caples. When I read his book and realized what he had, I was determined to learn it. For months I studied a chapter at a time. I would often "rewrite" his ads and letters, taking, say, an ad for a 1955 Buick and making it into a prospecting letter for my company. I learned (and continue to learn) from this master.

Comment

Over the years, I have heard many sales managers say, "Direct mail doesn't work." That's just a confession that they don't know how to make it work. Properly designed and tested, direct mail can generate very high-quality leads. It's especially valuable where the response rate to a phone/mail/phone-style call is very low. Normally, to make a standard direct-mail campaign work, you need a highly profitable item to sell, because it can cost as much as $100 or more to get a lead.

I once designed a campaign for someone in the financial services industry not too far from where I live. We sent out a thousand letters and received one response.

Profitable?

That one response was a very specialized client who generated more than $25,000 in revenue per year. Had we tried to call all of those people just to find that one, we would undoubtedly have grown discouraged and thrown in the towel. (I had a favorite towel as a boy. I kept it for many years. One day, my mother came to my room holding a garbage bag. She looked at me with a scowl. "You want me to throw in the towel, right?")

Web Drive

A web drive is a very important variation of the standard direct-mail campaign.

Instead of asking the recipient to call or return a coupon, they are sent directly to your website, preferably to a landing page.

At Bill Good Marketing, we do tens of thousands of direct-mail letters a month. We use letters instead of a lot of fancy color printing because of my own personal inability to be happy with something for very long. I like to mess around and test different things. If you invest some thousands of dollars into color printing, that's the end of your messing.

In the few years prior to the publication of this book, there has been a major change in the way many people respond to direct mail. Instead of sending in a lead card or calling an 800 number, they want to check out the offer and/or company more closely. They will do that by going to your website. We have created a series of landing pages that have all the programming in them to get people registered and record total number of hits. A letter might tell readers to go to www.billgood.com/bgm system. This is just one of dozens of landing pages we use to enable us to track results and generate leads. When people want our free offer enough to take the time to register, that tells us a lot about our list and about our prospects. When one campaign has run its course, we may use the same page with different text and other free offers.

Required Elements

1. Standard direct-mail letter
2. Landing page with capability to download promised info
3. Web-hit follow-up script

Background

We have always tracked the sources of our sales. In 2002 or so, we first noticed that a significant number of our sales were coming from web registration. What worked best was a combination of postcards and direct-mail letters. The postcards only directed people to the website. The letters always put the web offer in the postscript.

Comment

Major companies use all kinds of advertising to drive people to their websites. But small companies have limited resources. The good news about direct mail is that if your offer is a good one, you can build traffic. Once you capture the email address, you have a potential customer name that you can legally email.

Email

An email campaign is just a standard direct-mail campaign adapted to this medium. You can ask people to call you. The usual action is to provide a link in the email to a web page where they can get the material you offered in the message.

Required Elements

1. Email message
2. Landing page with link to information offered
3. Web-hit follow-up script

Background

With postage bills ever climbing, we all love the price of direct email. When early direct-email campaigns produced terrific responses, I thought the new marketing millennium had arrived. We used email a lot. But alas, spammers have virtually destroyed email as a lead generation device except where you have a pretty solid connection with the recipients.

Comment

An email campaign can provide the least-cost lead you will ever see. However, in today's spam-infected world, your biggest challenge is gathering email addresses of people who opt in. Without this, you have just joined the legions of spammers.

You can buy lists of names of people who have supposedly opted in. I wouldn't touch those if I were you. You will wind up getting your email blacklisted. So for now, just know that the names on your list must be from people who have voluntarily given you their address.

We frequently offer people something in exchange for completing a survey. We do a lot of surveys, and on our web resources page, which you can access with your personal password right from the book's home page at www.hotprospectsbook.com, you will find our current survey program. On the surveys, I not only gather basic demographic information but also can frequently get people to tell me about their business so I know in advance whether someone is likely to be a prospect.

Dripping

Dripping is a series of very low-key letters and/or phone calls designed to build or maintain an identity so that when the client or prospect is ready to buy, your name will be in first position.

Required Elements

1. Interesting information, generally written or an enclosure accompanied by a brief note
2. Business-reply envelopes (most of the time)
3. Ninety-day no-contact script

Background

Possibly the inspiration for dripping came from a true MDA (master drip artist), my youngest daughter, Jenny. When she was about five, we drove past a Sinclair gas station. They were promoting a "Dino the Dinosaur" or something. Jenny said, "Dad, I want a Dino." I was intent on heading some place or other and told her, "I can't do it right now, blah blah blah."

A few days later, we passed the station. "Will you stop so I can get a Dino?"

I replied, "Blah blah blah."

This happened a few more times. Each time, Jenny would just ask. Never any pressure. No wailing or carrying on. Not her style.

One day, as we passed a Sinclair station, she just said, "Today, Dad?"

All of a sudden I realized that this would go on until the end of time. I whipped the car into the Sinclair station, walked in, and bought the Dino. Back in the car, "Thanks, Dad." And I'm sure I earned a big wet kiss—and the lesson that dripping works. It doesn't take force, just pleasant persistence.

Comment

With dripping, we want to achieve "top-of-the-mind awareness" (TOMA)—owning the mental space your client or prospect devotes to the category of product or service you sell. When you have achieved TOMA, when your prospect is ready to buy, he or she will think of you.

Through the low-key phone calls made as part of dripping, lower-grade prospects or clients can be upgraded to hot, red cherry, or green cherry.

Dripping is normally done with clients (people who have bought something) or people who have already responded. However, I am familiar with several cases in which highly targeted groups of people were dripped and then, after some period of time, were contacted or simply sent in a reply.

Well over half of your new business could come from a well-dripped prospect file. So if you do not maintain contact, the number of new clients will be less than half of what it could otherwise be. Remember, people like doing business with people they know. A tasteful series of letters and low-key phone calls gives people the feeling that they know you, or at least that they know you better than they know the competition.

No-Key

If *low-key* means low pressure, then *no-key* means no pressure. So a no-key campaign asks for nothing.

Its primary use: build or strengthen an identity among your business associates so that they might realize what you do. When they have your kind of business to transact, they will call you. In financial services we have a new-identity campaign in which we repetitively send information regarding financial matters.

The simplest version of this campaign is to find an article or item of interest and write a handwritten note to your clients and prospects.

> *Dear Joe:*
> *Here's something I thought you would find of interest.*
> *Sincerely,*
> *Hyrum Smedley*
> *Beam of Light Financial*

Required Elements

1. List of business associates or personal connections
2. Commitment to continue this campaign for at least a year
3. Something of interest to send

ASSIGNMENT

On the Campaign Development Checklist, pick a style for the campaign you are developing.

16

Google Magic Tricks

Using the Greatest Search Engine
to Help You Write Great Letters and Scripts

> *. . . an offer you can't refuse.*
> —The Godfather

Wish I'd said it first, but oh, well . . .

When running a campaign, the offer you make needs to be seen as valuable enough to cause your clients and prospects to want more information from you.

The offer creates the action.

The headline of your letter, fax, or email can contain the offer. Sometimes it just attracts attention (BALD SPOT GROWING?).

The offer is what you will provide if people respond. You hope it's an offer they cannot refuse. If they can't refuse, you have found or created sufficient interest to cause action to occur.

Here's a classic headline: DO YOU MAKE THESE MISTAKES IN ENGLISH? It was written nearly a century ago. Variations on it run to this day. It obviously does not contain the offer.

The offer is usually something free (free report, free sample, trial subscription), a reduction in price, or a solution to a problem.

But if you just offer FREE REPORT, they've seen it before. Infomercials are filled with these offers. There is no intrigue or interest, and in the trash it goes. It could have been a really good opportunity, but was an equally bad headline.

In this chapter you are going to be thinking about your offer and creating some possible headlines or, for the telephone, opening benefit statement ideas. We are not yet going to be crafting the actual messages. The thinking part comes first.

HEADLINES AND OFFERS

Here are some samples of headlines and offers gleaned from a Google search for "sample direct-mail letters." Some are obviously better than others.

Headline: FIVE FREE CDs WORTH $600!!!
Offer: How would you like to save 20 percent on your computer purchases?

Headline: ANNOUNCING A NEW WAY TO DELIVER FLOWERS THAT DOESN'T HOLD WATER
Offer: Starter kit with money-back guarantee

Headline: TAKE THE WORRY AND THE WORK OUT OF HAVING A BEAUTIFUL LAWN
Offer: Free consultation

Headline: CUT YOUR COMPANY'S EXPENSES BY 30 PERCENT
Offer: Free month's long distance just for trying us out

Headline: THE LOAN TO END ALL LOANS
Offer: Extremely attractive interest rate

Headline: MANY PEOPLE THINK ABOUT INSTALLING A SECURITY SYSTEM. BUT ONE THING ALWAYS CONVINCES THEM: A BURGLARY.
Offer: Free security survey

As you can see, headlines can offer to save you money, solve your problems, and bring something new to your life.

The offers are for things that are free or at lower cost.

BENEFITS AND FEATURES

You have heard it said ten thousand times: People buy benefits. Stress benefits!

This is absolutely true.

Your product or service is loaded with features. Each feature has a benefit. As you plan your promotional message, it's essential that you understand the difference.

Benefits

A benefit is the perception of what a product or service will do for the buyer. It saves time. It saves money. It improves quality of living. It makes your wife smile. These are all benefits.

Joe Consumer might buy a laptop computer to increase his productivity, or he might buy it to save time.

You might have purchased this book because you felt it would help you make more money. Or perhaps you are under the gun from your boss to find more prospects. If you get more prospects, you get to keep your job. Or perhaps you felt that more prospects would enable you to get a promotion.

Joe buys a microwave. Why? He just doesn't have time to cook a conventional meal, so he buys it to save time. Perhaps he believes that some of the new microwave recipes will help him cook better dishes.

These are all examples of product benefits.

What enables a product to deliver its benefits? The features.

Features

A feature is some characteristic of a product or service that enables that product or service to deliver benefits to the buyer.

Using the same examples as above:

Joe buys a laptop computer with a 250-gigabyte hard drive.

Why does he need that? Joe is a graphic artist. The size of the hard drive enables him to store all of his music and artwork on his computer while making it possible for him to carry his critical files with him as he demonstrates his portfolio.

Here's another feature: the friendly computer salesperson says, "It has 2 gigabytes of RAM."

Joe's question should be, "So what?"

By having a lot of RAM, the computer runs much faster. Joe now doesn't have to sit around and wait while the computer lags in opening a program.

Consider this book: a feature of this book gives you the detailed information on list development. "So what?" you ask.

Answer: by being able to develop and manage good lists, you will be able to find more prospects and make more money. More money is a good benefit. A better prospect is also a good benefit. This book also contains detailed instructions on campaign development. Why? By knowing how to develop a campaign, you can deliver more prospects to your boss, definitely keep your job, and possibly even get promoted.

Got the idea?

At this point, if you don't already know this information cold, list several features of your product and their corresponding benefits.

FINDING INTEREST

You know what an offer is; you know the difference between a feature and a benefit. Now let's use these two tools to find interest.

Interest is our first requirement for a qualified prospect.

If he or she doesn't have it, we don't have a prospect of any kind.

With no interest, qualification is pointless. So here are the principles that, when applied, will enable you to find interest.

1. Clients and prospects buy benefits, not features. This concept should be so obvious as to require no comment. However, based on my own consumer experiences, very few salespeople truly understand what causes a prospect to buy. A few years back I wanted to buy a car for my then-sixteen-year-old daughter. The salesperson rattled off that the car has antilock this, power injection that, and a lot of other things that I'd never heard of and couldn't have cared less about. But I did know this: they were all features, and that's not what I was buying. What I wanted to buy was something safe that got excellent mileage, and was stylish enough that she would enjoy it and take care of it. The first two benefits were for me. The last one was for her. We didn't buy that first car. We bought the car from the salesman who immediately understood what benefits I was

looking for, and the benefits that satisfied my daughter—which subsequently included better speakers and a CD changer, too.

2. Clients and prospects ask questions about features, not benefits. This is odd, isn't it? We buy benefits but ask questions about features. "How many bonds in the fund?" or "How long has the manager been with the fund?" If a consumer buys benefits and not features, why does he ask questions about features and not benefits?

   I think there are two answers to this question. People ask questions about features because they need to know how the product or service delivers the benefit they want to buy. They also may need to know if the delivery of the benefit generates additional work or distraction. And perhaps more important, they don't want to appear a total pushover to the salesperson. They want to demonstrate that they are reasonably sophisticated and can't be sold a bill of goods (mine, but *not* based on my name). So they ask the most technical question they can think of to prove that they are analytical, not emotional, buyers.

   Here's where all of this is leading: if a person does not ask questions, you can be virtually certain he or she will not buy.

   Since most salespeople fill up their presentation with features, it leaves all but the most sophisticated buyer with nothing to ask. With no questions to ask, *they will not buy.*

3. Therefore, in your initial script, letters, and sales presentations, stress the benefits and withhold features so your clients or prospects can ask questions about the features if they are interested in the benefits.

BENEFITS/FEATURES EXAMPLES

Let's take some examples of benefits and features.

Let's go back to a car for my daughter. The benefits that I want are that it be safe, economical to operate, and that my daughter likes it. What are the features that support these benefits?

Certainly air bags and a solid construction would support safety, and more than thirty miles per gallon and low maintenance contribute to economy of operation. That takes care of my needs. But another benefit is that it must be stylish. She will ultimately be the only judge of that.

Let's suppose she needs a new car and I coincidentally receive the following call:

"Hello, Mr. Good, this is Bob Hammer at The Suave Dealership. Our new X5 is safe, economical, and very stylish. If you happen to be looking for a car for your son or daughter, I would like to take a second and run a few questions by you. Yes? No?"

Would I be interested in talking to this fellow? You bet.

Would I necessarily schedule a test drive? That might depend on his offer.

"Mr. Good, your daughter will love this car. Until the end of the month, we have an offer of an iPod docking station so she can listen to her music wherever she goes. It's normally three hundred fifty dollars, but if you were to come and at least look, it's yours if you buy her the car before the end of the month."

How do we pick the benefit, craft it into words, and then marry it up to an offer they can't refuse?

Unfortunately, this brings us to a tough question: How well can you write?

For most, this is a problem, isn't it?

You sell cars; you don't write copy.

You got a C– on your last English paper and hate the thought that you have to write something.

You might need a direct-mail letter and you especially need a telephone script. And they both better be up to professional standards.

Let's start with some facts. Most people in direct sales are not great writers, but most people in direct sales can rewrite.

If you have a good letter or script that may not quite fit, you can make it work. Correct?

So let's establish and work with this principle: *It's easier to rewrite than to write.*

Rewrite what?

Your headline, your opening benefit statement, your direct-mail letter.

How?

GOOGLE MAGIC TRICK

Let's just say that what you are looking for is a great headline or opening benefit statement.

Where can you find ideas that could be made to fit?

Google.

Do a Google search using the features of your product as the key search words. You can then quickly inspect how some of the best headline writers in the world handled these features.

Let's say you sell butcher knives. (I just bought some.) You sell to stores that cater to cooks.

The features of your product are:

- Sharp
- Durable
- Good grip
- Long lasting

Basically, these features are pretty much the same as any other knife.

So log on to Google and use the search string "Cutlery sharp durable good grip long lasting."

When I did this I was able to grab these web page headlines:

HIGH-QUALITY KNIVES AT A DISCOUNT PRICE!

SHARP ENOUGH TO BE IN A BLOODY HORROR FILM

LOVE THE KNIVES

THE SHARPEST CHOICE SINCE 1928

AN ALL-PURPOSE ASIAN-STYLE KNIFE THAT'S IDEAL FOR CUTTING MEAT, FISH, AND VEGETABLES

TRY THIS CUTLERY SET IF YOU ARE ON A HIGH-PROTEIN, LOW-CARB DIET

PERFECTLY WEIGHTED FOR PROFESSIONAL BALANCE AND CONTROL. IMPORTED.

Odds are if you sell cutlery to kitchen stores, you need to call on each store in your area. Let's assume, for the sake of argument, that the person you need to speak to is the owner, and like most business owners, is hard to reach. You need an appointment.

Here's your opening benefit statement:

Introduction: "Good morning. This is Bob Garfish with Slice 'em and Dice 'em Cutlery."

Opening Benefit: "Our smashing new display, Love the Knives, is generating an average increase in knife sales of about twenty-five percent."

Offer: "If we can set an appointment for me to show you our line in the next week, Slice 'em and Dice 'em Cutlery has authorized me to bring along a set for your personal use."

So what about this opening benefit and offer?

Good?

Probably. But we don't know, do we?

We need to test it. Maybe our competitor just came in ahead of us with a "smashing new display" that already increased knife sales.

Go back to your trusty word processor, redo your opening benefit statement and offer, and test it again.

ASSIGNMENT

Complete the "Google Magic Trick" step on your Campaign Development Checklist.

17

To Script or Not to Script

What you say makes a difference.
—Bill Good, age fourteen

I'm sure, by now, that you are just bowled over (mine) to know how many statements you grew up with that are mine. But what you don't know—at least not yet—is that I have a whole bunch of statements I haven't yet released. As I mentioned, when I was fourteen, I shut up. Don't get me wrong, I didn't stop coming up with great statements, I just kept them to myself. Instead of telling my mother or Sunday school teacher, I wrote them down. I trust that as I release these now, credit will be given where credit is due (mine). So I hope you enjoy the never-before-released statement I have chosen as the theme for this chapter. It also has a lot to do with our next subject. By the way, I almost used this statement when I asked the prettiest girl in school, Anne, for a date. I said, "You probably don't want to go to the hayride with me, do you?" She said, "You got that right." I almost said aloud, "Hmmmm. What you say makes a difference," but I squelched it and jotted it down instead. In my next attempt I said, "I have an invitation here to go to a party at Joyce's. Would you like to take a look at it?" She said, "When is it?" And you know the rest of the story (also mine).

Whether you advertise, attend trade shows, generate leads from the Internet, or cold-call, at some point in your campaign you will use the phone to qualify, set up an appointment, and possibly even close the sale.

Exactly what you say is critical; hence this chapter.

If you are going to have a campaign, at the very minimum you will need some words to say. So we have arrived at a critical juncture. You can keep doing what you've already been doing, which may or may not be very successful for you, or you can take your prospecting to the next level of professionalism.

Obviously you picked up this book with the hope that you might pick up a few tips that could help you achieve that level.

In this chapter I will help you with the scripts you may have found difficult to develop in the past. Developing your scripts (and letters) is a critical part of campaign development. Don't wimp out on me now! We're just getting into the good stuff.

YOUR MESSAGE COUNTS

Suppose you work for Beam of Light Financial Services and you call up a business owner prospect and say:

"Jack, this is Fred Smithers at Beam of Light Financial Services. We've got a terrific opportunity here. I want you to empty out your bank account, bring it down to the office, and we'll load you up. How's that sound?"

Frankly, with that message, I think Jack would be crazy to set foot out of his house, unless it was to come down to your office to punch your lights out. Quite obviously the words you say are important.

According to me, "What you say makes a difference."

The wrong words will stamp out whatever interest you might have created, whereas the right words will fan a spark of interest into a flame. Let's dig into the subject of the message. Your prospecting message is a very important variable. If you have an excellent list and yet you deliver a tired, boring message, your results will be both tired and boring.

Before actually getting into the mechanics of designing the message, let's talk about whether you should have a written script. Then we'll look at some important strategic questions that will help shape your words into a message that will provide outstanding results.

TO SCRIPT OR NOT

Very early in my sales training career, I encountered two phenomena that have always puzzled me. On one hand, there is no question that a well-written script gets better results on any list than no script at all; on the other hand, most salespeople would rather cut off a body part than use a script. So what exactly is a script?

By "script" I mean that every key word and key concept you should say to a prospect during a sales presentation is written down on a page. I do not mean that every single word is scripted—that would be impossible—but the key sections should be. Sometimes you will use all the key sections; at other times, one or another section will not be necessary. And you should always fill in the cracks with your own ad lib.

Since most salespeople would rather pay parking tickets than use a script, and since I believe a written script to be vital, let's look at both sides of the issue. Perhaps I can convince you that *a script is vital for the telephone contacts in both your lead generation and lead development.*

REASONS NOT TO USE A SCRIPT

At many of my seminars, I ask the salespeople attending to write down three reasons why it might not be a good idea to use a prepared script. I want you, the reader, to do that right now. Then I want you to compare your reasons with the reasons below. The ones I'll give are the same ones that crop up in every sales group I have ever worked with. It is amazing how consistent salespeople are, from one area of the country to another, from one company to another.

Sales managers take note: the items listed below are the reasons your sales crew will give you as to why they don't want to use a script. If you're big on scripts, you better know these well.

It sounds canned

By this, salespeople mean that the script sounds as if it is being read, not said. Who needs that?

It's "not me"

By this, most salespeople mean that the script isn't written in words they would use, and someone else's words make them uncomfortable. And they sound it. So naturally, since it's "not me," they don't want it.

It's not spontaneous

Surely an inspired, spontaneous presentation has more life and vitality than a forced-sounding, "canned pitch."

It makes me talk too fast

When people try a prepared script, they find themselves blabbering on at two hundred words a minute. And once again, the poorly written script takes the blame.

It's impersonal

Obviously, a presentation that is impersonal won't create a rewarding relationship between salesperson and prospect. Since the script is not written with any one person in mind, it is quite obviously impersonal.

It's inflexible

This is fairly obvious. A salesperson with decent verbal skills should be able to adapt his or her presentation to each individual rather than lose business due to an inflexible script.

I can't listen

People feel that when they're reading, they have difficulty listening. And everyone agrees you should listen to the people in your life, prospects included.

I get thrown off

One of the worst fears a salesperson has is getting thrown off a script and then groping around, at a loss for words. And that definitely can happen.

It's boring

Frankly, people just get tired of doing the same old thing over and over.

*　　　*　　　*

These are the negatives. I'll bet if you did what I asked and wrote down your reasons for not using a script, at least two out of your three are on my list! (Most likely all of them are.)

REASONS TO USE A SCRIPT

Now let's look at the positives. Take a moment and write down three reasons why it might be a good idea to use a prepared script. Here are the positive reasons salespeople come up with once they've given it a little thought:

You sound certain

If you have something to say, you'll sound as though you know what you're talking about. This will handle the "ah"s and "um"s and dead spaces you fear.

You can test

If you're using a different script on every person you talk to, there is no way you can tell what worked and what didn't work. You've got to hold all variables constant in order to test.

You cover all your important points

I can't tell you how many salespeople have told me that they have gone through their presentation only to learn that they have forgotten to get the prospect's street address or some other piece of qualifying data without which they don't have an order.

You can listen better

When you've got your message worked out, you can concentrate on what your prospect is saying.

You can make more calls

If ever there was a truth told, this was it. If your message is written down, you're more likely to stick to it. But if you start winging it, you'll thrash around until you have created a bloated message. And your bloat will take much longer to say. Thus a short, neat phone call becomes a blubbering, lumbering, twenty-minute, pit-polishing phone call.

Let's review the reasons not to use a script and see if I can't get you to look at scripts in a different light.

It sounds canned

Certainly many salespeople, when using a script, do sound canned. If you look at the bonus chapter at www.hotprospectsbook.com, "How You Sound," I show you exactly which speech elements cause a canned sound. Once you understand this, and once you have a good script, you can avoid sounding canned. You only need your personal password for the bonus chapters.

After all, there is a difference between script preparation and script delivery. Some of us may be good at developing a sales message. Others may be excellent at script delivery, and delivery of a script is really just a question of performance, isn't it? An actor does not create the script. He makes it come alive, and as more than one writer on the subject of sales noted, great salespeople are also great performers.

It's "not me"

This objection is obviously true. To the salespeople who complain "It's not me," I tell them "Be someone else." There is no reason why anyone should be restricted to one style of sales. Surely you would sell to New York lawyers one way and to North Carolina grain dealers another. If I'm giving my seminar in the South, I'll speak more slowly. I'll let my old North Carolina accent come out. But if I'm in New York City, I will adjust my speech, humor, and many of my examples (script, if you please) to a faster-paced audience.

It's not spontaneous

True, a script is not spontaneous. But the art in delivering a script is to know it so well that you can deliver it the thousandth time with the same spontaneity as the first. (Realistically, the first time you gave it and you explained the benefits of your product without a script, you probably stumbled through it and it didn't sound spontaneous at all. It probably won't even begin to sound good until around the hundredth time.)

It makes me talk too fast

This is a problem when using a prepared script. Many people, when they have the written word in front of them, act as if they haven't read aloud since the third grade. (Many haven't.) Instead of reading as they speak, they just fire away at a machine-gun rate. The only way I know to overcome this is to read the script aloud about fifty times. Then record it, and then compare a recording of the script with a recording of yourself speaking naturally. Force the script to conform to the way you speak as a human being, not necessarily as a salesperson reading a script. In the bonus chapter, "How You Sound," I show you how to mark a script for emphasis, inflection, and pacing. Don't skip it.

It's impersonal

If you just read the script and make no spontaneous comments, it will absolutely be impersonal, but that's not necessarily bad. There are only so many ways to qualify prospects for interest and money. There is no problem if you want to get off the script briefly to personalize it.

It's inflexible

A good script *is* inflexible. Any good script is designed to find a certain type of prospect. As you try to develop a script that will appeal to everyone, you will wind up appealing to no one.

Here is part of an inflexible script. We use it in prospecting for people who might use our system:

I have some important information available on our computer-based marketing system that could very well help you double your business or work half as much and do it in two years or less. May I send it to you?

Here's another example:

We've developed a marketing system to help a big producer get bigger. Am I talking to the right person, or should we part company at this point?

As you can see, both of these scripts are inflexible. Each is looking for a particular type of buyer. The idea behind the inflexibility of a good script is that you, as a lead generator, have set in your mind the kind of prospect you want, and you are going after that type of person. If the prospect does not meet your requirements, you find one who does. Remember, we're not trying to sell to everybody. We just want to sell to those who are interested, qualified, and with whom we want to do business. When your good script is good and inflexible, it will help you find the kind of prospect you're looking for.

I can't listen

You really can't until you've rehearsed the script. If you'll spend ten minutes to an hour reading your script aloud, over and over, you'll find that you can actually listen better because you won't be wasting mental energy thinking about what you're going to say.

I get thrown off

There is no question that you can be thrown off. I'll never forget a young man in Des Moines, Iowa, who was reading a particular paragraph of a script, got asked a question, forgot his place, and then began to read the same paragraph again. All the color suddenly drained from his face, and I heard him stutter, "I'm . . . not . . . doing a very good job. Suppose I call you back later, okay? Thankyouverymuch." (Click. Dial tone.) Remember, the system you're learning in this book contains an ejection seat. If you get in trouble, press the eject button!

It's boring

We did a study at Harvard and discovered, to everyone's surprise, that salespeople like making money. We then asked 4,085 salespeople: if you had a script that was making money for you, would you be bored? Three replied yes, they would be bored. On further investigation, it was found that two of these were independently wealthy anyway, and one was a part-time welfare worker who believed that money was the root of all evil. But the other 4,082 salespeople interviewed replied that they most certainly would not be bored.

What's boring about using a script?

Getting no results is very boring. When you find yourself getting bored, chances are you're doing something wrong and are not getting results!

TWO MORE REASONS TO USE SCRIPTS

The reasons salespeople give to use a script are all true. I would like to offer two more of my own.

Top salespeople use scripts

It may not seem as if they have their scripts written down, but they are. They're in their heads. If you ever have the opportunity to listen to a top salesperson give a presentation a couple of times, you will notice not just similarities but also identical passages. He or she has worked these words out over the years and wouldn't change them for anything.

Fairly early in my career I was fortunate on two occasions to sit through a seminar given by one of the top financial advisers in the United States. This was twenty years ago; he's still at it. When I heard his one-hour seminar the first time, I learned a lot, not only about his investment style, but also about seminar structure and design. It was brilliant. Then I heard it again. The thing that struck me the second time was that the speech was virtually identical to the first.

Over lunch at a conference in Reno, Nevada, I asked him, "John, don't you get tired of giving that same old seminar over and over again?" He looked at me as if I had just asked one of the world's most stupid questions. He answered, with a shrug, "If it ain't broke, don't fix it." (He quoted me without knowing it!)

He had his script. The idea of changing it was incomprehensible, especially since it put a lot of money in his pocket year after year after year. I've listened to other great salespeople. I find that they do the same thing over and over again. It's the new kid on the block (mine) who feels compelled to be unique and creative with each presentation. The old kid on the block long since tried that and found that some sets of words work better than others. And since he wanted to go to the bank instead of the welfare line, he stuck with the one that worked. Even if it causes brain damage to give the same presentation over and over again, year after year, he'll recover quickly enough when he cashes those paychecks each time.

Words create effects

This may seem self-evident. You were, I hope, taught by your parents that honey catches more flies than vinegar. To put it another way, it's

139

not just what you say, it's *exactly* what you say that counts. Consider these very slight changes in classic advertising slogans.

Burger King, original: "Have it your way." Slight modification: "Have it our way."

Visa, original: "Life takes Visa." Slight modification: "Life took Visa."

BMW, original: "The ultimate driving machine." Slight modification: "The best car."

Changing even a single word can alter the meaning and therefore the effect. If you have a good script, one that delivers predictable and profitable results, changing it is a sign of advanced brain damage. Don't do it.

YOU WILL USE A SCRIPT

As a final argument for using a written, word-for-word script, try this: if you're going to be making high-volume phone calls, there is no way, after the fiftieth call, that you will have failed to develop a script. It is impossible to make fifty rapid and unique phone calls. It won't happen. By the fiftieth call you will have a script, whether you intended to or not. And it will be one that you have settled into and, more likely than not, will contain such gems as "Mr. Jones, I was wondering if maybe . . ."

So you will use a script. The only question is, will you write it down in advance or just fall into it?

Now that the argument is settled and you are using a script, we need to discuss some basic strategy for the script. The questions I am about to go over will help shape your script. Please give very careful thought to these questions, my comments, and your own answers.

SHOULD YOUR OFFER INVOLVE SERVICE, CONCEPT, OR PRODUCT?

We've already defined your offer as something you give to clients or prospects in exchange for their response. Let's first define some terms:

Service: Something you can do for someone.

Concept: A group of related products. Blue-chip stocks, apartment buildings, and photocopiers are all concepts in the sense that we are talking about a product type— concept—instead of a particular product.

Product: Something you can write an order for. You can buy or sell a thousand shares of IBM; you can buy or sell the apartment building at 405 Fiscal Street; you can rent or lease a Xerox photocopier. These are all products.

In almost any industry, there is some choice about what to talk about on the first call. Take fire extinguishers. You could talk about a service—this would be a free home safety examination that would, most likely, end in finding that the prospect needs more fire extinguishers. Or you could talk about a specific fire extinguisher that you would like to sell or at least get an appointment to show.

WHERE DO YOU START? SERVICE? CONCEPT? PRODUCT?

My answer is *product*. A specific product. If you are selling fire extinguishers, talk about the fire extinguisher that sells best in the type of market you're calling, and do that even if you have an entire catalog full of fire extinguishers.

As a first thing to test, offer a free report, price reduction, or solution to a problem provided by a particular product. As a rule, you'll get better results that way.

With every company with whom I've worked, in every market, in every part of the country, I have been able to get better results talking about the *right product*. And that's true even for such service-oriented industries as life insurance. I have found that the more specific you make your first contact, the more likely you are to discover interest and qualification. You will also be more likely to get people to make up their minds one way or the other.

THE RIGHT WAY IS THE GOOD WAY

You have to get the right offer about the right product crafted into the right words in the right script and then call the right list to make it work.

If you cannot find a product that is profitable to talk about on the first call, then fall back and try a conceptual approach. And finally, as a last resort before using your list to line the bottom of your birdcage, try service.

If you really want to talk service, *first talk product*. It works. Just try it.

IF YOU ONLY SELL A SERVICE

If your product is a service, you're in deep trouble on this approach, right? No. Just sell it like a product. Suppose you sell a consulting service. Just package it so it has a fixed price and accomplishes a verifiable result. For $1,200 (or whatever) you will tell your customer what's wrong and what it will take to fix it. Or if you sell financial planning, sell the plan, not the process. If you sell janitorial services, sell clean buildings. If you sell carpet cleaning, sell clean carpets.

Take seminars, a product we sell. A seminar is really a packaged consulting service offering a solution that applies to similar businesses. While I deliver a service, I package and sell it like a product.

If you sell a service, figure out what the end result of the service is, then assign a fixed price to at least the first sale, and sell it like a product. I used to wonder why there was so little good material in sales literature on selling services as opposed to product. The reason, of course, is that those who have mastered service sales sell a service as if it's a product. There is no separate subject of selling intangibles.

ASSIGNMENT

No assignment! You get off easy. I just had to get you pointed in the right direction and committed to developing a good script.

18

The One-Story Elevator Speech

Before preparing a telephone script, you need to spend some time on one line of it.

It's the one statement you make when a prospect does not recognize your name. You have thirty seconds to do it. If it doesn't bite, the call is lost.

To help you with this, I've researched the "elevator speech."

An elevator speech is a presentation you should be able to give when you step onto an elevator with a great prospect.

On the first floor, Mr. Bigg says, "Good morning, Foster. What do you do?"

You were about to push the third-floor button, where you were going to see the assistant vice president of purchasing for Bigg Company. Instead you push twenty-four.

You've got less than a minute. What do you say?

Naturally, you slide into your well-rehearsed elevator speech, to which Mr. Bigg replies, "Very interesting, Foster. Do you have a card?"

Well done, Foster. The hours you spent perfecting your elevator speech just paid off.

An elevator speech should take no longer than one minute. And you do need a one-minute elevator speech. But we're not going to focus on that right now. What you need now is the "One-Story Elevator Speech." (To help you with your full-blown elevator speech, I have posted some updated recommended reading for you on the web resources page. You will need your personal password to access this page.)

Let's rerun our little scenario:

Assume you get in that elevator with Mr. Bigg, and he punches the second-floor button instead of the twenty-fourth. He turns to you and says, "Foster, what do you do?"

You've got time for one sentence. This one sentence needs to say who you are, what you do, then offers a benefit that interests Mr. Bigg enough to want to hear more. On a cold or even a warm call, this is often the sentence that buys you the time you need to make your opening benefit statements.

It's the sentence you say on the phone when your prospect says, "No, should I?" just after you said, "You know who we are, don't you?"

You've got one sentence. Make it pay.

"Frankenstein Wooden Stakes makes Teflon-coated stakes to drive into the hearts of vampires so they stay dead forever and don't come back as zombies."

How are we going to learn to write a great one-story elevator speech?

We'll start by studying some great examples, some of which were not written for that purpose, but should the authors have encountered Mr. Bigg and had a one-story elevator ride, these would have served perfectly. Next, I will extract a formula from them. Then you will write or rewrite one for your company using the formula. When the time comes to prepare your scripts, you'll already have this critical line.

If you want to find more such examples for your Google search string, use "elevator speech for a company." You'll find buckets of them. Most of the time, the first sentence is what you are looking for.

Here are the best I found:

My principal business is giving commercial value to the brilliant—but misdirected ideas of others.

—Thomas Edison

With the exception of Thomas Edison, who is no longer around to give permission, all are quoted with permission.

We create brilliant names!
—Phil Davis
Tungsten Brilliant Brand Marketing

We make magic happen!
—Abracadabra Event Planners
(Abracadabra Event Planners is a client of Phil Davis. He wrote the one-sentence description and provided the permission.)

I help small businesses and nonprofits tell their story to the people who need to hear it.
—Chris King
Powerful Presentations

To help you further with rewriting the samples above, I found an exceptional piece. It was published in the *Jewish News of Greater Phoenix*. Its author, Dave Sherman, president of Connection Pros, is obviously following the well-worn path of generating some publicity for himself and his company.

Check the web resources page for the entire article.

Quoted with his permission is his advice on constructing your one-story elevator speech.

Only focus on the benefits. When you ask most people what they do for a living, they have a tendency to ramble on and on about all the things their company does. Unfortunately, what they are normally rambling about is all the features that their company provides. The challenge you face is that no one really cares about the features of your business yet. They typically don't know anything about you and don't want to know that much about your business.

What people say when talking about their business is:

- Our company does four-color brochures.
- We provide financial services for small businesses.
- I buy and sell homes.

If you really want to grab people's attention, you must completely focus on what benefit you are bringing to them. Using the above examples, here is how to focus on the benefits instead of the features:

- Our company specializes in four-color brochures, so your company will always look great in print.
- We provide financial services for small businesses like yours so that someday you'll be a big business.
- I buy and sell homes so you can get the home of your dreams and not have to do all the work.

Here is the exact formula: company name (or "we") + what you do + so what?

Here's an example: ABC Financial Planners (company name) specializes in retirement and estate planning (what you do) so you don't run out of money before you die and your heirs, not your uncle, get what's left (so what?).

Here's the Bill Good Marketing speech: Bill Good Marketing develops marketing and office management systems so our clients can more easily create the time and money to pursue important goals in life.

ASSIGNMENT

Using the formula of company name + what you do + so what?, write a one-story elevator speech. You will need it in the next chapter.

19

Script Rewriting

How to Have Professionally Written Scripts
if You're Not a Professional Writer

Put your best foot forward.
—*Bill Good, age twelve*

In the sixth grade, all proper boys and girls took dancing from Mrs. Steed. I was not the quickest student, but once I got it, I was the best, winning many dance contests. My "jitterbug flip" pumped the air right out of the room.

For one samba routine, Mrs. Steed kept saying, "Lead with your right." I didn't know what that meant. I thought about it and then said, "Show me.'" She put her right foot forward. "Is that your best foot?" "Yes!" she explained. "So you put your best foot forward, correct?" And out went yet another soon-to-be famous statement.

When you are preparing a script, you most certainly want to put your best foot forward because you don't get a second chance.

Although I have never written radio commercials, I am sure it requires some of the same discipline that writing a telephone script imposes.

Both radio commercials and telephone scripts must be short. Each deals with voice only. A wrong word can blow either out of the water. Also, as with telephone script writing, I imagine it would be difficult to become a good radio commercial writer. If I had to learn to do it, I

147

would get hold of a collection of the best radio commercials ever written, and I would rewrite each commercial dozens of times, adapting them with every new pass to suit a different product or service. By so doing, I would learn the structure and form of a good commercial. I know I would never learn the art of commercial writing by just reading or listening to radio commercials. Nor will you learn how to write good telephone scripts if you just read this chapter. I will teach you the best way to learn how to write scripts, which is to rewrite them. In this chapter I will walk you through rewriting a phone/mail/phone-style first-call script. You can then apply your knowledge and hone your skills by rewriting any of the numerous scripts in this book and on the website for this book.

As you start rewriting this and other scripts, you will note that I have used some very direct questions. Don't worry about offending people with directness, since the only people you'll offend are most likely people who cannot make up their minds. By asking direct questions, we separate the fisherpersons from the bait cutters.

As you will see, the questions you'll be asking are normally closed-ended. A closed-end question can be answered with a yes or a no. It is point-blank, and in addition to weeding out the bait cutters, it will get rid of the bush beaters and the tire kickers as well. Remember, one definition of a pit is someone who cannot make up his or her mind. We want to find those people early, since the major killers of salespeople are not the ones who say no, but those who say maybe.

Important Note 1: Whether you use the telephone for lead generation or just lead development, you need the skills taught in this chapter.

Important Note 2: It's easier to rewrite than it is to write. So in this chapter, I will give you a tried and true script and teach you how to rewrite it. You will then be able to rewrite other scripts.

Important Note 3: If you registered properly at www.hotprospects book.com, your name, company name, and other info will already be merged with *scripts.doc.*

PHONE/MAIL/PHONE SCRIPTS

We are assuming you will be developing a phone/mail/phone script. So we will need two scripts: a lead generation script, for cold-calling; and a second-call, or more properly named, lead development, script.

Of course, you can write whatever kind of script you want. But we're going to work on this type simply because a phone/mail/phone campaign is very easy to launch and inexpensive to run.

HOW TO GET THE MOST
OUT OF THIS CHAPTER

I strongly recommend that you go to the chapter 19 downloads on our website and save *scripts.doc* to your hard drive. The password is bretgood. (Bret is my son.)

When you open the document, you will see that the first two scripts are "My Script Worksheet—B2B Phone/Mail/Phone" and "My Script Worksheet: Initial Contact Follow-up." We'll be working with the B2B Phone/Mail/Phone in this chapter. You will then have sufficient rewriting skills to work through "My Script Worksheet: Initial Contact Follow-up."

As you will notice, each of these documents contains much more material than you will use. The idea behind these worksheets is to adapt what you can use and delete the rest.

We will start with these assumptions:

1. You have a list to call. For our purposes, it should be a cold-calling list. In that way you can get good practice, as you may not always know who is the decision-maker.
2. For the moment, we are going to assume it is relatively easy for you to get through to the decision-maker. (The all-too-frequent exceptions to this assumption will be dealt with in "How to Make More Calls." This was discussed in my last book. I have placed the material on our website as a bonus chapter. It is accessible with your personal password.)

The end result of this chapter and its assignment is that you will have a complete script to test.

BEFORE YOU START:
WHAT YOU NEED TO KNOW

Someone (not me, because I don't agree) said, "Writing is ninety percent rewriting." For you, as letter and script rewriters, writing is 50 percent preparation, 10 percent writing, and 40 percent rewriting.

In this section we're talking about the 50 percent preparation, most of which involves writing things down that you already know so you can see them.

Here's your first assignment in this chapter:

1. If you wimped out on me earlier, go back to chapter 16, "Google Magic Tricks: Using the Greatest Search Engine to Help You Write Great Letters and Scripts," and study it well. Complete your assignment there. Write down your offers and your headlines.
2. If you were a complete loser and did not write your one-story elevator speech, do that now.
3. Write down the minimum qualifications that a prospect will need to purchase your product or service. I'm sure there are really more than the three I'm listing below, but these will serve us for now.

Need. Do they need or want your product or service? If you are selling an air filter for allergy sufferers and no one at the household suffers, don't waste your time.

Money. Do they have the money or the credit?

Decision-maker. Are you talking with someone who can buy?

Do these assignments now.

REWRITING GREAT SCRIPTS

Just to make sure you know what I mean by rewriting, here's an example:

Original for financial services. M/M_____, I have some important information for investors on what's called a tax-free municipal bond fund. Have you ever heard of one of these before?

Rewritten for computer sales. M/M_____, I have some important information for computer hardware buyers on our new Armadillo computer. Have you seen the ads we've been running on TV?

As you rewrite, I want you to pay attention to these rules:

1. No sentence should contain more than fourteen words. Long sentences are fine for school compositions, especially when you don't have much to say and need to pad. But they are not good for sales, which is spoken, not written. In spoken English, your listener can't go back to the beginning of one of these long, tortured sentences to see what you started out to say. Very often, in rewriting a script, you will find that you have produced a fifty-five-word monster sentence. Make it several shorter ones.
2. No technical words. Never assume that a prospect is as well educated as the salesperson. Most prospects might think a debenture (a kind of promissory note issued by a company) is something old people put in a glass of water on their bedside table each night. Edit out complex and technical words.
3. Don't talk more than fifteen seconds without asking a question. If a prospect does not get involved in the conversation, you've lost. Questions are the salesperson's tool for creating involvement. Also, they help you establish control. In section 2 of this chapter, you will see an example of using questions to control a conversation.

Another reason to ask lots of questions is, how else will you know if your prospect is still awake?

Finally, asking questions enables you to control what the prospect thinks about. If you simply stop talking, who knows what the prospect might think about? Your frequent questions don't permit mind wandering.

With these principles in mind, let's rewrite a script.

PHONE/MAIL/PHONE FIRST CALL

Make sure you have your *scripts.doc* document open to "My Script Worksheet—B2B Phone/Mail/Phone."

A phone/mail/phone first-call script is designed to find cherries. It is not designed to set up an appointment or to sell. We'll reserve that for the second call.

To find a cherry in your first call, offer your prospects some written information. Your offer should explain why they want the information. Ask if the prospects are interested. If they are interested, ask up to five qualification questions. One qualification question is almost *always* about money.

Here's the procedure we will follow: I'm going to take the script apart to make sure you understand why I did it the way I did. In several sections I will give you two or more examples. (These examples are reproduced in your worksheet.) As we work our way through each section, you will delete what you don't want, keep what you do, and rewrite what's left.

Section 1:
Identify the Decision-Maker and the Screener

Getting through to the right person is half the battle. To identify decision-makers today and get to them, you have to deal with at least three players. In some cases there is a fourth player: the savior. We'll talk about this person in a moment.

When you call a business, the first person who answers the phone is the receptionist. In a corporation of any size, the receptionist will not screen calls. His or her job is simply to route calls to their correct destination. In many cases, voice mail answers the phone. However, in most companies pressing "0" will get you the receptionist.

The screener is normally the second person you talk to, and you want to talk to the screener because your only other option will be voice mail. At this stage, voice mail is like being sent to purgatory, or worse, hell.

However, the third player is voice mail, which can be a wonderful tool *once you have established a relationship,* or a daunting hole to fall into if you haven't established meaningful contact. From the point of view of the lead generator, it's mostly a black hole, wall, barrier, pit, bog of despair—call it what you will. Most of what I have to say on the subject of voice mail is in "How to Make More Calls," which I have posted to the website. For now, you just need these three rules:

1. When you hit voice mail in making a first call (no screener, just a person's voice mail), disconnect. Keep on calling and try this number again when you recycle the list.
2. Until you have made contact with a decision-maker, the *only* reason to use voice mail is to persuade a decision-maker to look at material you are sending to his or her screener. Never use email without permission.
3. Once you have a relationship, it is possible to use voice mail to leave messages and to get calls returned. But without a solid prospecting or client relationship, voice mail is where salespeople go to die.

So when the receptionist says "Good morning, Acme Company," you have two script choices: (1) decision-maker name known, or (2) decision-maker name unknown.

In each of these I want to point out some important matters.

Notice the first line: "Hi!/Good morning/Good afternoon." (PAUSE)

That (PAUSE) is there for a reason. It will cause the receptionist, who may be handling two hundred to three hundred calls per hour, to break the routine a second and generally say, "Oh, good morning." Now you are talking to a person, not a machine.

"This is [first name, last name] with [company name]."

You are going to be asking for someone's name. It's always easier to get a name if you give one. Try it. "I need to speak to the person in charge of [area needed]."

Key words: "need to speak." Not "May I please." Being just a little bit emphatic will get you more names.

What about this line: "In case I get disconnected, what is his/her direct extension number?"

Basically you are building a quicker call-back list with this question. If you don't get the direct extension, you have to go back through the receptionist next time. Do it right the first time.

Once you have received someone's email address, *always* use email instead of voice mail.

You can store standard email paragraphs as autotext. To do this, you must use Word as your email editor in Outlook and have a rudimentary knowledge of autotext, which you can gain in about five minutes through Help in Word.

Example:

Bob:

That call from 801-555-1234 on your caller ID was me. Rather than make you write down a bunch of stuff from voice mail, I've written it for you.

It's time for your next order of armadillo burgers. We have a special on until Friday at noon. Call me.

Ralph.

ASSIGNMENT

Based on who you will be calling, delete two of the three choices in section 1 on "My Script Worksheet." Follow all directions there.

Section 2:
Get Through the Screener to the Decision-Maker

Once you get connected to the screener, we're going to use the principle "The person who asks the questions controls the conversation."

Controlling the Conversation

Who is controlling this conversation?

> DAUGHTER: Daddy, why does it rain?
> FATHER: Well, uh . . . tiny little drops of water get together and become big drops. They fall down.
> DAUGHTER: Why do they fall down instead of up?
> FATHER: Uh . . . gravity. It's gravity that calls them down to the Earth, sort of like you call your dog.
> DAUGHTER : But why?
> FATHER: Well, uh . . .
> DAUGHTER: How far is it to the moon?
> FATHER: Uh . . . it's . . . uh . . .

Look at how you have probably been approaching the screener.

> YOU: May I speak with Bob please.
> SCREENER: May I tell him who is calling?
> YOU: Foster Frankenstein.
> SCREENER: And who are you with, Foster?
> YOU: Frankenstein Wooden Stakes.
> SCREENER [with tinge of hostility]: And you are calling about?
> YOU: I'd like to sell Bob some frigging wooden stakes. [Click. Dial tone.]

Okay. Your manners are better than that. But that's what you've wanted to do, right?

Our basic strategy for dealing with screeners is:

- Get the screener's name.
- Answer the screener's questions first.

"Hi, Fran. This is Foster Frankenstein. I'm with Frankenstein Wooden Stakes. I need less than a minute of Bob's time to see if he would be interested in looking at our new Teflon-coated stakes. Easy in, easy out. Would you connect me, please?"

ASSIGNMENT

Fill in the blanks in section 2.

Section 3:
Introduce Yourself to the Decision-Maker—
Engage with a Question to at Least Buy the Time
to Make Your Opening Benefit Statement

Your buyer, and every buyer, is programmed to instantly reject your offer. You could call and say, "We're running a sale on five-dollar bills. They're four bucks each. Interested?" The immediate response: "We're not interested."

We have to snake around that programmed response. You'll do that by introducing yourself and asking a question that diverts the attention from the usual response.

Here are some choices: (a) "Does the name [company name] ring a bell?" or (b) "You know who we are, don't you?" or (c) "Can you hear me okay on this phone?"

My personal favorite is (c). If you raise your voice and belt it out, you'll always get a yes. It may even seem illogical. But it diverts perhaps better than any other. With it, one of the others, or one of your own, you've bought fifteen seconds for your opening benefit statement.

Who is M/M?

When you get your decision-maker on the phone, your first line reads:

"Is this M/M_____?"

So who is M/M?

It's Mr. or Ms.

According to Judith Martin, who writes under the pen name "Miss Manners," when addressing women at work, use Ms. and the name the woman has built her professional reputation on. This may be a maiden name, a previously married name, a hyphenated name, or some other name. Miss Manners refers to this as "The Conservative Lady's Solution." Should you have occasion to call her at home, ask how she wishes to be addressed. According to annual *New York Times* surveys of marriage names, more and more women are opting for "Mrs." and their husband's last name. This demonstrates to teachers and others that they are a married couple.

On a further note, use Mr. or Ms. until you have asked and received permission to use a first name or a nickname.

ASSIGNMENT

Decide which of these statements you want to use. Delete the other two. You also can leave them all in and try them until you decide which works best for you. Or use another such statement. Please note: insert your elevator speech where it says, "One-Story Elevator Speech Goes Here."

Capture Attention/Make Offer/Qualify for Interest

You've got fifteen seconds. In that time you must first capture attention by offering your best benefit. To make certain you understand features and benefits, read the first sentence below and circle the benefit.

"I have a *free* special report for you on how the Bill Good Marketing System can help you stop procrastinating and start prospecting. It's called 'A Prospecting Strategy for the "Do Not Call" Era.' May I send you a copy?"

This one is twelve seconds.

Here's the formula:

- Offer something free.
- Assert that it will help them achieve a major benefit.
- Clarify what you're sending.
- Ask for interest.

Take another example. You work at a temporary employment agency. You have been assigned to call five thousand small businesses in your metro area. You must reach the business owner.

"I have a *free* special report for you on how Ace Temporary Services can help you cut your personnel turnover. Having to start all over again is, as you know, very expensive. May I send it to you?"

You work for Big Bucks Retirement Planning. You are calling business owners who have been in business twenty-five years. Their big challenge is getting the equity in their business into a retirement account.

"I have a *free* special report on how Big Bucks Retirement Planning can help you craft a plan for your retirement. This could be very important in case you cannot sell Frankenstein Wooden Stakes. Naturally, you are banking that you will, but what if you don't? May I send it to you?"

Here's where your assignment from chapter 16, "Google Magic Tricks: Using the Greatest Search Engine to Help You Write Great Letters and Scripts," comes in. You need your best benefit. You Googled it. Rewrite one of your offer statements here or the one on the "My Script Worksheet." When you've written it, time yourself. It must be fifteen seconds or less, preferably twelve to thirteen.

ASSIGNMENT

Rewrite "Capture Attention/Make Offer."

Qualify

Assuming the prospect does not want the report, the party is over. "Thankyouverymuch" and move on.

Once you have established a minimum level of interest, you need to do some qualifying.

Depending on your product or service, you will need to establish:

1. Need
2. Money
3. Decision-making capability
4. Time

I am reproducing below the "Qualify" section of "My Script Worksheet." I've added my commentary so you can see how these questions relate to the four requirements above.

Excerpt from My Scripts Worksheet, with Comments

So I can make certain we have a possible fit, let me ask a few quick questions. You've been a financial adviser for how long?

For the most part, if the person is brand-new, we don't want to waste time. They don't need our product at this point in their careers. But there are a couple of exceptions. So we continue.

And you have how many clients?

This tells me a lot. If they have fifty clients, for the most part they don't need what we have. They can do it on note cards.

In addition to referrals, what other methods are you using to develop new business?

If someone is using seminars or cold-calling or direct mail, they have a major problem keeping up with all the leads. Lots of stuff falls through the cracks. Big need.

Ballpark, with fees and commission, revenue should be in what range?

We really need someone generating at least $150,000 a year, preferably $200,000.

How familiar are you with the Bill Good Marketing System?

This tells me what kind of name recognition we have. If they say "not," it will be a slower sale.

For a single user, the system is [$X.00] which includes preparation, training, and implementation. If you like what you see and want to proceed, would [$X] be a problem at this particular time?

Do they have the money?
Because we sell to individual financial planners, when we get one to the phone, we know we have the decision-maker. In a corporate sale I would always ask, "What is the process by which you make a buying decision?"

ASSIGNMENT

Using my questions as a model, develop your own set of four to five questions to establish need, money, and decision. Note the green cherry option. If the prospect cannot make a decision now, find out when he will be able to do so.

Commitment: The biggest issue is time. I want to get the prospect committed to look at my material. So I will spell out how much of a commitment I need and then ask for it.

ASSIGNMENT

Rewrite my commitment statement so it's yours.

20

Lead Generation Letters

How to Have Good Letters

Even if You're Not a Good Letter Writer

It's easier to rewrite than it is to write.
—Bill Good, *age forty-three*

This is probably the last of the famous statements I held back. I was researching whether it was realistically possible to teach a financial planner how to write a direct-mail letter. After running a class on the subject, I concluded that this was not possible, at least in a reasonably short time. So I created some fill-in-the-blanks letters and discovered they could easily fill in the blanks and make other changes. I was talking to one of the graduates of that course and told him, "Bob, it's easier . . . to do a lot of things than write a letter." I got the idea, and I held back . . . until now.

I am not going to tell you that you will become a great letter writer as a result of reading this chapter. I will, however, tell you that if you take the time, you will become a good letter rewriter.

There are at least two styles of lead generation campaigns in which a letter, fax, or email is required.

Mail Only: This is the classic direct-mail-style letter. Send it to a targeted list, make an offer they can't refuse, and wait for the phone to ring, the mail to arrive, or for people to register on your website.

Mail/Phone: Here you send (generally) a letter, which may include a response request. Even it does include such a request, you plan on following up with a phone call three to five days later. This type of campaign can generate hot prospects on the first contact.

In both campaign styles you need a letter. The style of the letter in both is the same.

While we will be focusing on lead generation rather than lead development in this chapter, you will need the same set of rewriting skills. Even if you do not plan to use the mail-only or mail/phone campaign, read through this chapter and prepare a letter anyway. Who knows? Maybe it will open up a new area of lead generation for you.

RULES OF THE REWRITING ROAD

First let's cover some of the general principles of direct mail.

1. Prefer long letters to short letters

This is the most controversial rule. It flies directly in the face of common sense.

People are really busy, right?

They don't have time to read long letters, right?

So a letter should be no more than one page, right?

Oh yeah? Who says so?

While I do claim credit for many of today's famous statements, I cannot claim this. That belongs to the author of the bible on direct-response advertising, *Tested Advertising Methods,* John Caples.

When I first read Caples's book—and any professional in direct response has not only read it but consumed it—I came across his statement about long letters.

It sounded ridiculous—absurd, even—but I decided to test it. I became a believer in long letters, not as an article of faith, but by testing.

Why do long letters work better than short letters?

One theory is that if you can hook someone who has a base level of interest in the benefit you are offering, they will read at least some of the letter. They may jump around, catch a subhead that piques their interest, read that part, jump to the PS, then pick up the phone and call.

There are other theories, but there is no point in going over them now. You can believe or disbelieve all you want. But the only way to find out for sure is to test the concept for yourself. Testing, of course, is the heart and soul of *any* kind of advertising that solicits a response.

2. *Always* use the name of the recipient at least twice in the body of a letter

This is a really simple rule, and it means exactly what it says. You may think the reader will know his or her name is inserted in the letter by a computer. Absolutely true! But so what?

What seems to happen is this: a prospect gets a letter, and as he or she is about to throw it out, his or her own name catches the eye and forces the person to read a little more. Once again, don't believe what I say. Try it for yourself.

With any decent database program, you can insert various fields into the body of letters.

3. Use a catchy headline to get people to read your letter

Let's talk about headlines. Why do newspapers and magazines use headlines to start an article? To capture your attention! If a newspaper, say, *The National Enquirer,* to name a modern master of headline writing, just presented text with no headline, people would not have an easy way to decide what to read and what to skip.

Consider these gems:

CSI WIFE CLAIMS HUBBY'S UNDERWEAR PROVES HIS INFIDELITY
WIFE KILLS HUBBY TO COVER UP SHOPPING DEBT
VALENTINE'S DAY PRESENT . . . 3 SHOTS TO THE HEAD

We certainly won't be on the same plane as *The National Enquirer* when it comes to sensationalism. But we certainly do want to use headlines to draw attention to our letter, and then we want to use subheads to help keep the reader engaged. Later in this chapter, use some more Google magic tricks to get great headlines.

4. Use short sentences; use short paragraphs; use subheads and boldfacing to break up long letters

As you rewrite your own lead generation letters, pay special attention to this rule. Long sentences are hard to read. Short sentences are easy to read. If you have long letters that do not get broken up by subheads, people will find it more difficult to get the information they are interested in. Once again, in a long letter, people tend to read a little here, jump to there, and based on this spot-reading method, decide what to do after that. As you review your letters, make certain you have followed this rule. It makes a big difference.

5. First paragraph: no shortage

Sometimes, in rewriting a letter, you may get stuck on the first paragraph. I want to pass on to you a piece of advice I got from my first writing teacher. I was working on what would become my first published article, which was published in *Barron's Business and Financial Weekly*. At some point I realized I was stuck on the first paragraph. I told her, and she said, "That's ridiculous! There is no shortage of first paragraphs. There are billions of first paragraphs. I want you to write ten first paragraphs right now. Start!" That's what I did.

The first several paragraphs I wrote were junk. Then, at about number six, I nailed it.

If and when you get stuck on a first paragraph, write one right after the other. The first few may be completely worthless. Not a problem. Keep going. You'll get it right.

If you're still stuck, get some first paragraphs from a newspaper or a magazine and start rewriting them, taking care, of course, to avoid plagiarism.

What to Rewrite

Let's get busy with our rewriting. The first question is, What are we going to rewrite?

We will focus on four sources:

1. *Letter formats.* These are fill-in-the-blank letters that will provide three different styles for you to rewrite. I will go over one of these formats in this chapter. You can download them from the chapter 20 download page. The password is nicci. (She is my oldest daughter.)
2. *Brochure copy.* One great advantage you have in creating lead generation letters is that you probably have some excellent copy on brochures created by your marketing department or by the companies that make the products you sell. Here's what the folks in marketing will hate: you will often get better results from using the copy of a brochure as the basis for a letter than by sending out the

brochure itself. At a minimum, always use the "Here's the Info" letter when sending out printed information.

I will show you how to use brochure copy later in this chapter.

3. *Great direct-mail letters.* In *Tested Advertising Methods* there are lots of great ads and letters. In addition, there are books full of direct-mail letters. If you search Amazon with the phrase "direct-mail letters," you will find a bunch of books with titles like *Greatest Direct-Mail Letters of All Time.* You can take any one of these letters and use its style and format to create your own. This method gets us closer to writing instead of rewriting. However, you are better off *mastering* letter formats and rewriting brochure copy before you begin rewriting direct-mail letters.

4. *Previous direct-mail letters:* I'm not going to use precious pages in my book to reproduce some of my own letters. Instead, in the download page for this chapter, you will find a series of letters that were rewrites of one of the best letters we ever sent out. You will enjoy these letters because they deal with "monster rabbits." No famous statements here, just good fun . . . and lots of money.

LETTER FORMATS

The best way to show you how to develop a letter from a letter format is just to do one. On the left-hand side of the page, you will read a selection from a letter format. On the right-hand side of the page I will give you the text of a letter I have created from the letter format. I have picked a completely absurd topic to show how easy it is.

I have reproduced this example from the previous edition of this book because a rewrite produced real income. A few years after my last book was published, I received a letter from a financial adviser who discovered a company about to close down its pension plan. Employees were receiving a lump sum. He rewrote my ridiculous letter and sent it to employees of the company. He opened many new client relationships and raised many millions of dollars in new investment assets. Who knew that my silly example would pay off that well. I should have asked for 10 percent. Oh well.

In the example that follows, we will use the "Good News Letter" format (named after me, of course). The two other formats are "Here's the Info" and "Feature/Benefit." You can download all three from the web page for this chapter.

Print the "Good News Letter" format and have it available as we do what it says.

Good News Letter from Bilge Water Pumps, Inc.

1. The Heading

February 30, 2099

Captain Joe Blow

Garbage Scow Unlimited

3900 East Main

Long Island, New York 33098

Where an entire batch of letters is being printed for mailing over several days, omit the current date.

[Current Date]

[Full Name]

[Company]

[Address]

[City], [State], [Zip]

WE PUMP BILGES FASTER

Your headline goes here, centered, occupying two lines if necessary

Dear Captain Blow:

Use a formal salutation for mass mail—Mr. Ramirez. Use familiar salutation for clients and prospects—Steve and Edie.

2. Announce you have good news

Captain Blow, how about some good news for a change?

Choose one of the following:

- I have some good news for you, [Salutation].

- [Salutation], how about some good news for a change?

- Most of the news you read in the papers these days is bad, isn't it, [Salutation]? Well, how about some good news?

- Last month I had some good news for you. This month? Surprise! More good news, [Salutation].

- How about some more good news? [Firm name] has just (announced/made available) [what it is].

3. Tell what the good news is, using the strongest benefit

My company, Bilge Water Pumps, Inc., has done it again! In time trials, our SR90 Bilge Water Pump proved that we pump more bilges faster than any other pump!

Use following prompts to stimulate your thinking

The top . . .

The best . . .

One of the best . . .

One of the newest . . .

One of the top . . .

[Well-known company or person] has done it again.

[Well-known company or person] is still doing it.

For the (third/seventh/etc.) (year/month/quarter) in a row . . .

4. Give three benefits the client or prospect can expect from ownership or from receiving the free information

To you, Captain Blow, an SR90 Bilge Water Pump could mean:

- Fifty percent more bilge water pumped into the ocean than with any other pump.
- Less rot due to stagnant water because it gets pumped out faster.

  or

Choose one of the following:

To you, [Salutation], this means:

- [first benefit]
- [second benefit]
- [third benefit]

or

- More time off in port because you won't have to be supervising your staff cleaning the bilges. It will be done before you dock.

Captain Blow, ask yourself this question: Am I interested in less bilge water and more time off in port?

If you answered yes, then send in the enclosed information request form, and I will send you the details. Fair enough?

Sincerely,

Catherine Burger

Senior Vice President, Bilge Water Pumps

[Salutation], you'll see how:

- [first benefit]
- [second benefit]
- [third benefit]

5. Call for action

Choose one of the following:

[Salutation], ask yourself this question: Am I interested in [primary benefit]?

If you answered yes, then send in the enclosed information request form and I will send you the details. Fair enough?

or

To find out more about how you can [get primary benefit], just put the enclosed information request form in the enclosed envelope and send it back to me.

or

If you have an interest in [investment type] with [best benefit], call me, or just drop the enclosed information request form in the mail, and I will rush the information to you.

6. Signature

Sincerely,

[Name]

[Title]

7. Information request; reinforce with PS

PS. If you're thinking, "I don't know," just do it! Imagine, instead of pumping bilges when you hit an exotic port, you get to go ashore and enjoy! So send in the information request form, okay?

Complete info on how to construct the information request form is on various letter formats that are on the download page to this chapter.

Choose one of the following:

Dear [initiator name]:

Sounds interesting. I want to see some additional information on [what it is]. Please drop it in the mail for me.

or

I'm not interested in [what it is], but I'd like information on: _____.

Let's look at the completed letter on the next page.

COUPON DESIGN: THE SECRETS

One of the most important parts of a direct-mail letter is the information request form. This is not just a form for someone to request information. It is a vital persuasive tool to get the prospect to act. No way should it be dull and boring.

One of the first jobs I held when I left grad school was working as the assistant to the publisher of a small magazine. My boss during that time would edit my articles and in the process helped me drop my academic style. My somewhat unglorious job included fetching her lunch from the deli across the street or typing personalized renewal letters for her magazine. There were only about two thousand subscribers. But since each paid $700 per year to subscribe, they were entitled to some special treatment. She insisted that each letter be typed individually, with no mistakes.

Every renewal letter we sent out had a separate coupon enclosed. To

February 30, 2099

Captain Joe Blow
Garbage Scow Unlimited
3900 East Main
Long Island, New York 33098

**Headline uses
18-point bold**

WE PUMP BILGES FASTER

Dear Captain Blow:

Captain Blow, how about some good news for a change?

My company, Bilge Water Pumps, Inc., has done it again! In time trials, our SR90 Bilge Water Pump proved that we pump more bilges faster than any other pump!

To you, Captain Blow, an SR90 Bilge Water Pump could mean:

• Fifty percent more bilge water pumped into the ocean than with any other pump.

**Name used
three times**

• Less rot due to stagnant water because it gets pumped out faster.

• More time off in port because you won't have to be supervising your staff cleaning the bilges. It will be done before you dock.

Captain Blow, ask yourself this question: Am I interested in less bilge water and more time off in port?

If you answered yes, then send in the enclosed information request form, and I will send you the details. Fair enough?

Sincerely,

Catherine Burger

Catherine Burger
Senior Vice President, Bilge Water Pumps

**Use 12-point
Times New Roman
for body text**

PS. If you're thinking, "I don't know," just do it! Imagine, instead of pumping bilges when you hit an exotic port, you get to go ashore and enjoy! So send in the information request form, okay?

order a renewal, all the subscriber had to do was send back that coupon and a check in the reply envelope we provided. My boss told me many times, "When you design a coupon, always write yourself the letter you would like to receive if others wrote letters in response to yours."

That was the best advice I have ever seen on how to write coupons. After many more years in the business I have discovered a few more rules to supplement that advice:

1. Print the coupon on a separate page. Unless there is a compelling reason not to use a separate sheet of paper for the coupon (also called the information request form), you should put it on a separate page. Your computer can be set up so it prints the information request form right along with the letter.

2. Use a business-reply envelope. In some industries, stand-alone cards work fine, but not in financial services. Every time we have tested stand-alone reply cards against coupons inserted in business reply envelopes, response rate falls. People seem to be reluctant to put any information about their finances on a postcard. I know I am. However, you may still want to use a stand-alone business-reply postcard. If you use this method, you can print three to a page with a laser printer. However, the side of the card with the "Postage will be paid by" stuff should be printed by a commercial printer, who will have all the Postal Service–approved artwork. The permit must be printed according to Postal Service requirements, or they will not accept it. Then you've just wasted a whole lot of money on a mailing that may or may not have had spectacular results.

3. A very important point in designing a coupon is how many choices to offer. You might think that you should have lots of choices in your coupons. If a prospect is not interested in your main offer, perhaps he or she would be interested in something else. If not that, what about this?

    Following this logic, you could wind up with a laundry list instead of a coupon. I have found that when you have more than three choices on your coupon, your response rate goes down. What should the choices be?

    a. The prospect should be able to request information directly related to the offer in your letter. This choice should restate your offer and be humorous and urgent but never boring.

        Example: Absolutely! Bill, I am very interested in your system. I have done my part by requesting information on

170

how I can double my business or work half as much. Now it is time to do your part. Please rush me the information on the Bill Good Marketing System.

b. Give the prospect the ability to request information on something else, and leave it up to the prospect what he or she wants.

    Example: Nope! I'm not interested in your system, but I am interested in _____.

c. Provide a place for your prospect to refer you to someone he or she may know who could use information about your product or service.

There is nothing set in stone about these choices. You could certainly make a compelling case for one or two more choices or even fewer. Just know that too many choices will bury your letter in the recycling bin.

4. Use a merge field to insert the prospect's name where the signature would normally go in a letter. The easier it is for your prospect to slip the information request form in the business-reply envelope, and mail it without having to fill in name, address, and phone, the more people will respond. Make it easy for them by doing the work yourself.

Remember: the coupon or information request form is a vital selling tool; don't let it be dull or boring.

The information request form I developed for Bilge Water Pumps is on the next page.

REWRITING BROCHURES

Some of the best copywriters in your industry would be delighted for you to use their material in your direct-mail letters.

Let's follow our fantasy example of Bilge Water Pumps.

I did a Google search for "commercial bilge water pumps" and came up with BJM Pumps.

Assume for the moment that you sell BJM pumps. You could start a letter to Captain Blow right out of their "KZN Series" online brochure (http://www.bjmpumps.com/data.htm). I've italicized their text so you can see what I've added.

Salutation to you, just like a letter.

Information Request

Dear Catherine:

☐ YES! I want more time on port. Rush me the information on the SR90 Bilge Pump.

Give option to receive info by e-mail.

Please:

    ☐ E-mail it to me at: _____

    ☐ Mail it to me.

☐ I'm not interested in the SR90, but I would like some other information about:

Please:

    ☐ E-mail it to me at: _____

    ☐ Mail it to me.

☐ I'm not interested in anything now, but a friend might be. Send me an e-mail at: _____ and I will send you the name.

Best bet to follow up is my cell phone. Of course, you won't catch us at sea but I will return the message when we hit port. Reach me at: _____

We need some way to call him since he is often at sea.

Captain Joe Blow
Garbage Scow Unlimited
3900 East Main
Long Island, New York 33098

By inserting name of respondent, it's easier to respond.

Dear Captain Blow:

Our KZN Heavy-Duty Submersible Slurry Pump with agitator is the choice of industries that face the most difficult pumping. *Barge and tank cleanout* is right up there with other tough pumping jobs like *lime slurries, slag pits,* and even *silt removal.*

Now, I truly don't have a clue what I just said. But it reads pretty well, doesn't it?

You could actually take the information in this brochure and slide it into any of our letter formats. So if you are struggling with a letter, the solution may be no further than your nearest Internet connection.

Caution: I am in no way recommending that you rip off someone's hard work. Always ask for permission to use someone else's copyrighted works. But I can almost guarantee that if you sell products produced by someone else, your vendor will be delighted to grant that permission.

PRIZE-WINNING DIRECT-MAIL LETTERS

The best (which means the most profitable) letter I have ever written was a rewrite of a 1938 letter I found in a book of great direct-mail letters. Unfortunately, that book grew legs and I cannot tell you how to get it, as I don't know where I got it myself. However, libraries and bookstores are filled with books that have lots of great direct-mail letters in them.

The particular letter I adapted was a letter about launching a longitudinal trip around the world. Whoever hired it to be written had put together an airplane trip that would fly over both poles. I took their concept and wrote a letter about the Bill Good Marketing System and how its purchase and implementation was like a journey, not around the poles of Earth but into outer space.

My mail room staff hated that letter because it was seven pages long. Ugly! It also made millions of dollars for my company. Today that letter is part of the proposal we send to anyone interested in our system. If you want to see a seven-page letter based on a rewrite, download "The Journey." You will find it in the section for this chapter.

PREVIOUS DIRECT-MAIL LETTERS

Once you begin producing lead generation messages, you will discover that one of the best sources for new material is the letters you have already written.

At my company, we have copies of every letter we have sent out since about 1991. A good part of our preparation for sending new direct-mail letters is to study the letters we have already sent.

One thing we do extremely well is to keep records on which letters have produced our best sales. Such careful record keeping lessens our chances of sending out a letter that has failed at least once before.

HEADLINE WRITING: WHERE TO FIND GREAT ONES TO REWRITE

Since headlines are such an important part of a lead generation letter, I want to round out the information I gave you in chapter 16, "Google Magic Tricks: Using the Greatest Search Engine to Help You Write Great Letters and Scripts," with another example.

More moons ago than I care to think about, I took a comedy writing class at UCLA. In this class my teacher taught us how to do what he called "switching." This was where we learned how to keep the buildup of a joke and switch or change the punch line to something else. Then we learned how to keep the punch line and switch the buildup. Finally, he made us switch the buildup and switch the punch line, which, of course, gave us an entirely new joke! We had to write hundreds of jokes using this switching technique. The switching technique basically taught us to master the form of a joke as opposed to its words.

Well, with headlines, "same drill, different day."

If you want good headlines for your letters, it's best to get ten or twenty headlines that deal with your topic and then switch them.

Let's take a company that sells advertising, RSVP Marketing. We'll say hello to them now. You will get to know them later in a case study. Features of their product include low-cost, postcard, targeted audience.

So I Googled "advertising + low-cost + postcard + targeted." I got a bucketload of headlines. From just the first two pages, I copied down these:

- High-Response Marketing with Low-Cost Postcards
- Low-Cost Marketing Trends 2007
- Eight Low-Cost Advertising Ideas
- Postcard Marketing: Low-Cost Visibility
- Strictly Business: Promotion Through Postcards
- Low-Cost Marketing Methods Sometimes Produce the Best Results
- Seven Tips for Successful Postcard Marketing
- The Seven Principles of Postcard-Marketing Success
- Postcard Power
- Low-Cost, High-Return Approach

Let's switch some of these around:

- Postcard Power: Low-Cost Marketing Methods Sometimes Produce Best Results
- Strictly Advertising: Low-Cost Visibility with Postcard Power

You get the idea.

All you have to do is play around with your search terms. Pick *features* of your product. Google them. If you don't immediately get good ideas, fiddle with your terms, sticking with various product features.

THE DISCIPLINE: INTRODUCING THE "REWRITING A DIRECT-MAIL LETTER" CHECKLIST

I have some good news and some bad news for you. Which would you like to hear first? (age ten). You want the good news? Great! I have made up a checklist to walk you through rewriting a letter. If you follow these steps, all will be well. The bad news is that the process of rewriting is a little more complicated than just picking up a letter format or brochure and rewriting it.

There is a discipline to the subject. By following this discipline over and over, you have an excellent chance of getting it right. You can get the Microsoft Word file of the complete "Checklist for Rewriting a Direct-Mail Letter" from the download section for this chapter.

Can you skip some of these steps? Sure. But the first few times you create a new letter, follow them, would you?

21

Testing

Testing, testing. 1, 2, 3, 4
—Bill Good, *age fourteen*

When I was in the eighth grade, my science teacher was a little bit hard of hearing. I was doing a chemistry experiment. As a matter of fact, I was doing four of them. He asked, "What are you doing?"

I replied, "Testing." He put his hand up to his ear to indicate he could not hear me. "Testing," I replied louder. He shrugged and still could not hear. Pointing to each experiment, I said, "1, 2, 3, 4."

A Google search shows 990 million results for my phrase "Testing, testing, 1, 2, 3, 4"—which just goes to show you how these statements got out of hand.

You have written your campaign. You have defined your objective, crafted your offer, and created at least one script and a letter or, if you are planning a phone/mail/phone campaign, two scripts and a letter. You've done your list homework. You're ready to go.

Well, almost. First, I want you to review two bonus chapters, "How to Make More Calls" and "How You Sound," from my previous book. The knowledge they contain is critical for the long-term success of your campaign.

You can access these with your personal password. All your good work can go down the drain if you don't crank out the calls or if you sound like a monotonous encyclopedia salesman. These two chapters cover these two critical variables. They are variables in that they can affect the outcome of your campaign, sometimes dramatically.

The most important thing you can do when you launch your campaign is to keep good records. We recommend that you set up a file folder for each test.

In the folder, note what the list is; put in a copy of the script and/or letter; and, if a telephone campaign, note the time of day you are calling.

If this is a direct-mail campaign only, you should probably not send less than two thousand letters.

If you are doing a telephone-only campaign, call for an hour or two—three at the most—and then reevaluate your results. If you are not hitting into the profitable range, change one variable, most likely your sound, script, or the time of day you are calling. Then retest.

At this point in your study, get the campaign going. Don't wait until you finish the entire book. Start generating leads.

While you are waiting to get that first lead, go ahead and get to work in our next section and learn what to do with it. We call this lead development.

BOOK THREE

Lead Development

22

Lead Development

The Missing Link in Sales

Lead development is the process of increasing the interest level of a prospect to the point where the financially qualified prospect is interested enough to set an appointment to talk to the salesperson and thus becomes a hot prospect.

Hot prospects are what this book is about.

Lead development also may pick up a lead that has cooled off and reheat it. If the prospect is not on the salesperson's calendar, it should be in the lead development process, not the sales process.

Salespeople are worth $1,000 an hour in gross revenue when meeting with and talking to interested, qualified clients and prospects.

In practically every company I've ever heard of, lead development is assigned to the salesperson. In many companies, salespeople are expected to generate leads. Some of them barely have time to sell, committed as they are to generating and developing prospects.

But what if you (or your sales team) dealt with hot prospects only? What if the newer, less skilled people dealt with the red cherries, greenies, info leads, and pitch-and-miss, all the while coping with pits and jerks?

The lead developer is the missing link in sales.

So let's look at where lead development fits in an overall process of selling your product or service.

THE LEAD DEVELOPMENT PROCESS

Once again, let's review our definition of sales:

Selling is a step-by-step process intended to increase the desire to own the benefits of a product or service to the point where the desire outweighs the fear of change.

Lead generation finds prospects.

Lead development increases their interest to the point where they will talk to a salesperson.

The salesperson further increases interest while decreasing fear of change to the point where desire outweighs the fear of change. At that point the sale will occur, many times even without the nudge of a good close.

Lead development owns the big middle part of the sales process.

Question: What if a prospect is not willing to set up an appointment?

Answer: Then you don't have a hot prospect. You have to increase desire and/or reduce fear of change. When you get a hot prospect, the appointment will set up.

Question: How do I increase desire?

Answer: You have to show the prospect how the benefits of your product or service align with the prospect's visions and goals. As Frank Bettger, author of *How I Raised Myself from Failure to Success in Selling*, put it: "Show a man what he wants and he will move heaven and earth to get it." First key to sales: know what he wants. Then show it to him.

Question: How do I know what they really want?

Answer: Ask as many questions as possible.

In chapter 25, "The Sales Profile," I will thoroughly cover the issue of the sales questionnaire, or profile, as I prefer to call it. You are not going to find what someone really wants just by popping off a question or two. "What are you trying to achieve?" will get an answer, but in many cases not the real answer or certainly not the only one. You have to ask lots of questions about visions, values, and goals. Going through these questions with both your clients and prospects will get you the answers you're looking for.

And you will know it when you find it.

Questions are the answer.

Question: What about fear of change? How do I reduce that?

Answer: There are three ways. First, in both your corporate brochures and web presence, stress the longevity and stability of the company. Second, use countless success stories from people with characteristics as similar as possible to your prospects. Present these in conversation, in writing, on CD, or on the web.

Finally, constantly monitor your lead developer's telephone presentation to verify that he or she is upbeat and demonstrates complete certainty in what he or she says. (Study the bonus chapter "How You Sound.")

LEAD DEVELOPER TOOLS

To increase desire and decrease fear, the lead developer has a toolbox that should include:

1. Product knowledge—able to quickly respond to any of the twenty-five questions most frequently asked of salespeople in your company. Fewer things will shake confidence more than a salesperson who is uncertain of the answer to a critical question.
2. Lead classification cheat sheet—see chapter 5, "Lead Classification by Temperature."
3. Sales profiles—see chapter 25, "The Sales Profile."
4. Lead development messages—see chapter 24, "Lead Development Messages."
5. Lead development scripts—see chapter 23, "Lead Development Scripts."
6. Corporate brochure—shows stability, longevity, good standing in the community. (Constructing a corporate brochure is beyond the scope of this book. If you don't have a good one, create a white paper. You can use the white paper template from the downloads section for chapter 26, "Client and Prospect Education.")
7. If necessary, personal brochure, résumé, references—you need these if you are selling a personal service.
8. Educational materials—white papers, brochures, articles about different aspects of your product or service that can be sent to prospects and/or posted to your website. The best way for relatively new lead developers to provide educational materials is to direct prospects to the resource that will answer their questions. Later, as you become more skilled, you can do the education right on the spot.
9. Testimonials—letters, recorded phone calls, or video available on CD or streamed from your website.
10. Website—this is a given in today's marketplace. Not having a website where people can check you out is like not having an address or phone number.

As you can see, there is some complexity to the process of developing a lead, not only in doing it, but also in understanding it.

Here's the plan so you can both do and understand it:

In chapter 23, "Lead Development Scripts," I will cover lead development scripts. In chapter 24, "Lead Development Messages," I will cover a very important tool for the lead developer, lead development messages. In chapter 25, "The Sales Profile," I'm going to get into the lead developer's most important tool, the profile. Then in chapter 26, "Client and Prospect Education," I'll address the issue of educating the prospect.

In chapter 27, "Case Study: Developing a Lead," I will pull together most of your tools with a case study.

Finally, in the last chapter, I'll show you how to double your sales by . . . well, stay tuned.

23

Lead Development Scripts

To develop a lead, you have to make contact. If you cannot reach a prospect by phone, you are dead in the water. If your follow-up message is not spot-on, you might as well never have called.

To help you make contact, you have two tools: your lead development messages, which we will cover in the next chapter, and your lead development scripts. In this chapter, as the title indicates, we will cover lead development scripts.

We use the scripts to call back existing prospects and develop them to a higher category. You should download these now. The password is max. (He's my newest grandson.)

MYSTERY APPOINTMENTS

Before getting into the various lead development scripts, I want to voice my objections to a type of appointment setting practiced in many industries that I call the "mystery appointment." If it sounds bizarre, trust me: this is the way many major firms teach their salespeople to prospect.

In setting up a mystery appointment, you don't let the prospect know anything more than your name, your company, and that you have some important but unspecified need to see him or her right away. Basically, you just bully your way in the door. Those who work for the offending companies will recognize this style instantly.

M/M_____, this is Joe Doakes with Acme Company. I have a few new ideas I'd like to share with you. I'm going to be in your neighborhood between four and six o'clock on Friday. When can I see you?

Another version is practiced extensively by multilevel marketing companies whose distributors are explicitly told not to tell a prospective distributor *anything about the meeting*. Here's how one of these conversations might go. (And this is for calling your friends!)

FRED: Jack, it's your old fishing buddy, Fred.
JACK: Hey, when we going?
FRED: I got someplace else I want to take you and Alice.
JACK: What you got in mind?
FRED: It's something I think will be very important for you and Alice. Suppose I pick you both up at seven o'clock Thursday evening.
JACK: What are we going to do?
FRED: That's exactly what I'm going to show you. Thursday at seven?
JACK: Yeah, I guess.
FRED: Great! Thursday at seven. See you then.

One multilevel distributor I know went to pick up "Jack," found all the lights on, the TV on, dinner on the table, and no one home. I wonder why.

Here's a promise: if you trick your friends into seeing you, you might wind up with a few customers but fewer friends. Tricking people is just bad manners, and bad manners are bad business. (Hmmm. Possible future famous statement here.)

Instead, take on faith, for now, that in the time you spend driving out to see one of these mystery leads—or anyone else you have forced yourself on—you can sit down at the phone, run a phone/mail/phone campaign, find five or ten excellent prospects, and then set up some quality appointments. So no bully tactics. And no mystery, please.

OVERCOMING "I DIDN'T GET IT"

The most important lead development script is the red cherry callback script. When recontacting a red cherry lead, developers most often run into a very specific problem that must be successfully overcome.

Here's the problem: last week you sent some information to a red cherry; this week you call her back.

This is how the all-too-familiar second call goes.

FRED: Jackie, it's Fred Smithers over here at Acme. How are you?

JACKIE: Fine.

FRED: I sent you that information last week. Did you get it?

JACKIE: Doesn't ring a bell.

FRED: Remember the big package? Brown envelope?

JACKIE: Oh, yes. I've got it. Haven't had time to look at it yet. It's about number six down from the top.

FRED: When do you think you'll get to look at it?

JACKIE: Try me next week sometime.

Let's do a triple whammy handle on the "I didn't get it/I didn't read it" problem. You'll probably never stamp it out entirely. But we can sure cut down on it.

Here's what we'll do:

1. Mutilate the material you send out. By "mutilate" I mean write all over it, circle items, draw arrows, and so forth. If you do this, I promise you, your prospect is far more likely to read it.

2. When you send out the information in the first place, you can actually dispense with the new red cherry message (unless you are using email). Instead take your business card, flip it around, upside down, and backward, and write on the back, "Here's the information I promised." And sign only your *first* name. Then, using a paper clip, attach the card to the *upper right-hand corner* of the mutilated material. Make up a package as I described, put it in an envelope, open the envelope, and notice what you have to do to see who sent it.

   When the information arrives, your prospects will open the envelope, see your first name on the back of the card, won't have a clue as to who you are, will then have to take the card off, read it, and then, staring them in the face in the other hand, are your hand-written notes with phrases like "Read this" or "See page 9" in orange or some other prominent color. The prospect will now read what you've highlighted and perhaps the rest. Plus, by forcing your prospect to get physically involved with your business card, you've also had the opportunity again to let him or her know who you are. Repetition. Repetition. Repetition.

   Remember, you didn't send the prospect information because you care if he or she reads it. You needed to send it to establish who you are and to prove *through your actions* that you're not a high-pressure salesperson and are, therefore, safe to talk to.

3. When you make your red cherry callback, *bypass* whether the

prospect received or read your material. Never ask, "Did you get it? Did you read it?" Instead say, "I sent you that material last week, but before I recommend you get involved, there are two or three questions I would like to check with you. Do you have a moment or two?"

REWRITING THE RED CHERRY CALLBACK SCRIPT

Like the other script, your red cherry callback appointment script is made up of distinct parts. We'll go over them one at a time. I recommend that you download the *Lead Development Scripts.doc* and go to work. In case you've been a slug and haven't downloaded it yet, run, don't walk, to www.hotprospectsbook.com. The password is chloe. (She's my granddaughter who, when asked at age five what she wanted to do when she grew up, replied, "I'm going to save the world." Go for it, girl.) Find the script labeled "Red Cherry Callback Script" and work with me step-by-step. When you're done, you will have a red cherry callback script tailored just for you. More important, you will have had even more practice in script rewriting.

Here goes with the red cherry callback script:

Introduction and Bypass

By "bypass" I refer to the technique whereby we ignore completely whether the prospect received or read the material sent. Here's how you do it:

"May I speak with M/M____, please? M/M____, this is [first name, last name] with [Company]. I sent you that information last week, but before I recommend you get involved, there are two or three points I would like to go over with you. Do you have a moment or two?"

Please note: I didn't even remind the prospect what the information was about, since I really don't care if the prospect remembers getting it. All I care about is that by accepting the material from me, the prospect is now obligated to discuss it. With the introduction and bypass in place at the beginning of the second call, you should hear a lot less of the "I didn't get it/I didn't read it."

A note of warning: While some red cherries being called back will immediately upgrade to hot prospects, please don't expect everyone you qualified last week to make an appointment for this week. Here are some very broad rules of thumb that you can apply. About 20 percent of the people you talk to will be too busy right at the end of your introduction. Another 20 to 30 percent will blow you away long before you get to your appointment close. But if you do it right, you should be getting one or two appointments from last week's red cherries. Another one or two prospects will require additional information (still red cherries), and you'll wind up downgrading some to green cherries. None will downgrade to info lead status because for them to have been a red cherry, you had to have qualified them. The info lead category is for first contacts only. As you develop and work your pipeline, you will get more hot prospects from your pipeline than from fresh red cherry callbacks. But it takes time and consistency of approach to get your pipeline to this point.

ASSIGNMENT

Review the Introduction and Bypass section of the script. You may wish to make some changes. I cannot imagine what they are, as these lines are as close to perfect as you will see on this Earth.

Introduce Your Company and Yourself

If you work for a very well-known company—an IBM, a Merrill Lynch, a Bank of America—you don't need to spend any time telling your prospect about your company. These companies do an extraordinary job for you. But suppose you work for Pterodactyl Computers. Unless you happen to be very well-known locally, you could have a real problem.

You will solve *part* of that problem by sending some information about you and/or your company when you send out the requested literature. And in the scripts below, I will give you several different ways to sell yourself or your company, depending on what information you sent.

Here are the rules: If your company is unknown, tell your prospects a little about it. If you are doing lead development, also sell the sales professional. If your company is known, and you, the salesperson, are doing your own lead development, sell yourself.

I learned these principles when I first started my business. My practice was to go out on a sales call, make the presentation, and then go directly to a coffee shop to analyze what I had done. A number of patterns began to emerge. One of them was that when I would get near the close, the prospect would say, "Who are you again?" And I would have to present my credentials all over again. So I began experimenting with giving my credentials at different points in my sales presentation.

Here's what I now believe: the best places to present your credentials or those of your company are close to the beginning of the second call and again at the beginning of a sit-down sales presentation.

Here are some examples of how to introduce your company and yourself.

Seminar Sales

Mr. Jones, let me first tell you just a little bit about who we are and what we do. The name of the company again is Bill Good Marketing, Inc. My name is Bob Hammer. We specialize in training salespeople to find hot prospects. In your industry, we've worked with such companies as _____, _____, and _____. I would imagine that if you did get interested in one of our seminars, you would want to check with some of the other people in your industry who have used us. Is that correct? [Response]

We practice the team approach here at Bill Good Marketing. My job is contact management. I find people who could be interested in attending one of our programs and get them in touch with the right person at a time that works for you both. Normally, when the time comes to make a decision, you'll be speaking with Jim Sellers, who has been here a lot longer than I have. Does that sound fair enough to you? (What's your prospect going to say? "No that doesn't sound fair"? Notice how I am following the rule of speaking no more than fifteen seconds without asking a question.)

Financial Services (Doing Own Lead Development)

Since we've never met, I'd like to tell you a little about myself and the kind of work I do. My name, again, is Bob Hammer. I specialize in [info sent], tax-advantaged investments, and retirement planning. I'll answer any questions you have and stay in touch with new ideas and needed information. But I recognize that you're probably busy, and I'll respect that by keeping my calls brief and to the point. Does that sound fair enough to you, M/M_____?

Unknown Generic Company

In the materials I sent you, I enclosed some information about [company name]. I highlighted a couple of points, specifically [first point] and [second point] [offer restated]. Did you have any questions about us?

Pterodactyl Computers Example

In the materials I sent you, I enclosed some information about Pterodactyl Computers. I highlighted a couple of points, specifically the technical expertise of our staff and the fact that we've been right here helping people get more computers for their money for twelve years. Did you have any questions about us?

Remember: people like doing business with people they know. Since you have never been introduced, let's now take care of that. In reality, a salesperson with, say, one hundred accounts has one hundred part-time jobs. If you were applying for a part-time job, you would, of course, tell your prospective employer something about yourself. So let's do it here as well. The effect is magic.

Also, the "sell yourself or your company" step is very important to start establishing a professional image. You'll need this image to get your prospect to answer detailed and sometimes very personal questions. We will cover question asking in detail in chapter 25, "The Sales Profile." But for now, just know that getting the prospect to give you true answers to detailed questions depends in large measure on whether you are able to establish some degree of professionalism early in the relationship.

ASSIGNMENT

In "Sell Company/Self Intro of Red Cherry Callback Script" section in *Lead Development Scripts.doc,* rewrite it so it is yours. I have included several examples. As with other script development forms, delete what you don't want. When complete, each section should take no more than fifteen seconds and each end with a question.

Bridge to Profile

After introducing your company and yourself, you'll need a transition to get smoothly into the questions you'll be asking.

I call this transition "bridge to profile." It answers the question "Why are you asking me all these questions?"

Generic Company Intro 1

If our companies are going to do business together, it's important that you consider us more than just a company that [what you do]. Our best clients value their relationship with us because we not only provide them with [restate what you do], but we can also provide valuable insight to help them reach their other goals and improve their profits. We can do that because we take the time to really get to know you, your business, and your marketing. But we cannot complete our mission to [again repeat what you offer] unless I have a detailed understanding of how our service/product might fit into your company. So I do need to ask you some fairly detailed questions, okay?

Here's a generic and a rewritten example of a shorter bridge. **Please note:** in these we're running a quick check to see if we have a hot prospect.

Generic Company Intro 2

To make sure our Widget 2000 is exactly the right widget for you, there are a few questions I would like to run past you. We can do that in one of two ways. You can set up a time to come down to the showroom, or I can spend a few minutes by phone with you right now. Which way would you like to proceed?

Rewrite 1: Thundermobile

M/M_____, to make sure our new Thundermobile is exactly the right car for you, there are some questions I would like to run by you. We can do that in one of three ways. You can set up a time to come down to the showroom. Or my boss, Rock Ironweed, can grab a car and come give you and your husband a ride. If neither of those work, I can also spend a few minutes by phone with you right now. Which way would you like to proceed?

Rewrite 2: Financial Services

For me to do a good job for you over time, I'll really need to know more about where you are financially, how you got that way, but most important, where you want to be in the future. We can do that in one of two ways. We can set up a time to get together, or I can run some questions by you right now. How would you like to proceed?

ASSIGNMENT

In the *Lead Development Scripts.doc,* section "Bridge to Profile," rewrite this section and throw away what you don't want.

The Profile

The guts of the red cherry callback script is a profile. That's coming in chapter 25, "The Sales Profile." You will be developing a series of separate questionnaires when you get to that chapter.

Even though there are thousands of products that can be sold and tens of millions of questions that can be asked, there are broad rules that apply to anyone developing leads.

1. The first two or three questions should be questions where the answers don't matter. These questions simply get the prospect comfortable answering questions. For example:

   a. Let me just make sure I have your address correct. I have you down at 405 South Main Street. Is that correct?
   b. And your position is vice president of materials acquisition. Correct?
   c. Normally, what's the best time of day to reach you?

   None of these questions is critical, but each plays a role in getting the person into the *flow of answering questions.* The pattern you want to establish is you ask, they answer.
2. Ask less personal, less confidential, or less sensitive questions first.

The lead developer should focus on questions that ask for facts. These are certainly less personal than some of the other questions that can and should be asked.

For example, you sell envelopes. Your prospect uses them:

How many envelopes do you normally use a month?

Two colors or four?

Do you use a standard #10 envelope or an odd size?

The salesperson then asks the "soft questions," those that deal with evaluation, opinion, expectations, and change.

What do you most need from an envelope company other than top-quality envelopes at competitive prices?

Why did you ask us to bid on this job?

Normally the lead developer first completes the profile that I have named the "Basic Qualification Profile." If the lead developer doesn't get any strong interest signals, he or she should slide into "Status Quo Profile." You will learn all about these in chapter 25, "The Sales Profile."

3. Ask enough to generate your best interest signal, which is a question back to you. If the prospect has not yet asked you any questions, just keep asking questions. This may take several calls and meetings.

Call it the salami technique if you want. We just take a small slice at a time rather than going for the whole thing. If you try to grab the whole sausage, people will resist. Ask for a little bit at a time.

I'm not going to cover anything else now on the profiling section of the red cherry callback. When you have completed the assignment to develop your sales profile in chapter 25, "The Sales Profile," you'll have all the tools you need to make this all-important call.

Let's continue with the rest of the script.

The Close

The close for the appointment is actually quite easy. If you really have a hot prospect, you just ask. If you've done a good profile, the questions have worked some magic on the prospect's mind. They've actually created interest, so we really don't need too many techniques for closing for an appointment. We ask the prospect if he or she would like to get together and talk about it, and the answer will generally be "Sure."

We do, however, want to be just a little bit more elaborate. So we'll use a closing formula I call the ABC close. You can use this to close for anything. But our interest here is to get an appointment with a qualified and interested prospect. (By the way, some Old School sales trainers used the phrase ABC to indicate "Always Be Closing." I think this is junk. The close is simply that part of a presentation that asks for a commitment to act. The entire presentation is not made up of closing, as this statement indicates.) Here's what the ABC close is all about:

A is for Action

A close always involves an action. You don't want the prospect to just *think* about anything, you want him or her to *do something*. So on the first step of our close, we'll recommend an action. Here are some examples of action steps:

Mr. Jones, I think it would be an excellent idea if you brought your last two years' tax returns down to my office.

Mrs. Smithers, why don't you pull together all of your insurance policies?

Or, to your grandson,

Justin, my strongest recommendation is that you clean up that pit we used to call the TV room.

B is for Benefit

To make certain that no good prospect gets away at this point, stress a benefit for taking the action you have just recommended. Even restate your original offer. Here are some benefits for taking the actions recommended above. I have put the benefits in italics.

Mr. Jones, I think it would be an excellent idea if you brought your last two years' tax returns down to my office. Very possibly, I can show you a way to *cut your taxes significantly*.

Mrs. Smithers, why don't you pull together all of your insurance policies? There's an excellent chance I can show you how to get *more coverage for the same amount you're now paying*.

Justin, I think it would be an excellent idea if you cleaned up that pit we used to call the TV room. By doing that now, you have a *faint chance of seeing daylight this weekend*.

C is for Commitment

After you've told the prospect what you want him or her to do and have given a good reason for doing it, go immediately—without pause, without passing Go, without collecting $200—to the commitment question. Here are some complete closes, with the commitment portions in italics.

Mr. Jones, I think it would be an excellent idea if you brought your last two years' tax returns down to my office. Very possibly, I can show you a way to cut your taxes significantly. *I have a spot on my calendar on Thursday at four, and I'm also free Friday morning at ten. Which of those would be better for you?*

Mrs. Smithers, why don't you pull together all of your insurance policies? There's an excellent chance I can show you how to get more coverage for the same amount you're now paying. *I have to be out your way next Wednesday evening. I have a time available at six-thirty and again at eight-thirty. Which looks better to you?*

Justin, my strongest recommendation is that you clean up that pit we used to call the TV room. By doing that now, you have a *faint chance of seeing daylight this weekend. Would you like to start now, or in thirty seconds?*

ASSIGNMENT

In "The Close" section, fill in the blanks and rewrite as necessary. Now, that's a reasonable assignment for a close, isn't it?

Requalify (Your Hot Prospect Is Not, in Fact, Hot)

A minority of red cherry callbacks will go straight through to the appointment. So if it becomes apparent during the call that you don't have a hot prospect, what are we going to do? Whine? Sniffle? Hardly.

If our red cherry callback does not produce a hot prospect, we need to see what kind of prospect we do have. So here are some requalification legs for your script. As a rule, start the process by requalifying as a red cherry. If it becomes apparent you don't have a red cherry, requalify as a greenie. If no go as a greenie, you have to decide whether to pitch. If you can't find any interest at all, well, you had what I call a "false cherry," which I'll define as a pit wearing a vinyl cherry skin.

Remember, when you "pit" the prospect, you basically just return him or her to the mass-mail list from whence he or she regrettably came. When you pitch, this means it's someone you want to do business with but can't get it done. So we send a letter and place them into the drip process (see chapter 28, "Dripping").

Requalify as a red cherry: Is there any additional information I can send you, M/M_____, anything that might interest you enough to keep talking at this time?

Requalify as a greenie: M/M_____, let me ask you this. Is there a time in the future when you would better be able to consider my offer? [Response.] Terrific. Suppose I add your name to my mailing list. I will stay in touch until [month]. Meanwhile, if you have any questions, you let me know. Okay?

Pitch-and-miss: M/M_____, would you like to receive information from us from time to time? [Response.] Great! Here is what we'll do. I will add your name to our mailing list and then every so often I'll touch base to see if conditions have changed. Fair enough?

ASSIGNMENT

In the requalify section, review the three requalification paragraphs and revise if necessary.

After the Close

The appointment is closed. Now let's really firm it up. You can do this with a number of simple questions:

1. We will be meeting at the Ditchwater Café at 405 Swan Lake Lane. Would it help if I sent you a map?
2. Do you have a pencil handy? My name again is Catherine Burger. My phone number is 555-4444. If there is any problem with three o'clock next Thursday, will you give me a call?
3. Very good. I'll see you next Thursday, and you have a nice day, okay?

ASSIGNMENT

Almost done with your red cherry callback script. In section 7, rewrite Cat Burger's "post close." It can be almost any three or four confirmation-type questions.

EVEN MORE SCRIPTS

Sorry, we (meaning you) aren't done yet.

Among the remaining scripts you will need are:

Red cherry follow-up: A lead that is still a red cherry and has not up- or downgraded.

Green cherry follow-up: You have been in touch with this person through the drip process. You need to smoothly call, ease into some questions, and see if you can upgrade to red cherry or hot prospect.

Phone drip: This is the script you use for your pitch-and-miss leads.

These and other scripts are all part of the lead development scripts. Make sure as you develop to think through the examples I've posted and rewrite them until you have a script you are comfortable with.

24

Lead Development Messages

I've already told you the origin of "The more things change, the more they remain the same." I actually came up with it twice, and to this day, I do not recall which incident made it famous. So I thought I would share the second incident with you as well.

One night we had gone to some stupid school play. One of the characters kept changing clothes and becoming another character. But it was the same kid. I commented, "Mom, it appears the more that kid changes, the more he remains the same." My sixth-grade teacher, Mrs. Parker, actually misunderstood what I said and quoted me as saying, "The more things change, the more they remain the same." So sometimes you get it right by getting it wrong. Whatever the case, while change is the dominant factor in a prospect file, the messages are the same.

So you see the truth of my famous statement.

Part of developing a lead is keeping your name squarely in front of the prospect as he or she goes through the development process.

A lot can happen as you compete for mental shelf space.

While the telephone is your most important tool for moving the prospect up the temperature gauge, what you send by letter, fax, and email preceding or following most every contact is very important.

So let's identify a set of written communications (emails, faxes, and letters) that we will call lead development messages.

WHAT ARE LEAD DEVELOPMENT MESSAGES?

No matter which campaign generates a lead, you need some kind of message when someone becomes a lead for the first time.

It may be as simple as a note scribbled on the back of your business card, or it can be a full-blown written proposal. Today these written communications can be sent by email, fax, or letter. For convenience sake, we'll use the term "message" to refer to these different formats.

In managing a prospect file, the one constant is change. People who were less interested become more interested. Those almost ready to buy are now not interested or won't be interested for six more months. Your prospects move up and down our temperature gauge and, of course, frequently bail out altogether.

Let's call these movements on the temperature gauge lead category changes.

Examples:

A red cherry becomes a green cherry.

A pitch-and-miss becomes a red cherry.

A red cherry heats up and sets up an appointment (hot prospect).

A hot prospect quits returning phone calls and becomes a pitch-and-miss.

Whenever appropriate, use a category change as a reason to send a message.

Why?

Because it's good manners.

And quite frankly, it's also another socially acceptable way to keep your name in front of your prospects.

It is the lead developer's job to maintain contact and increase the interest until a prospect is hot, at which point he or she is turned over to the salesperson.

Use impeccable manners and meticulous follow-up by sending the right message to the right person. When you do so, your prospect lists (red cherry, green cherry, info lead, and pitch-and-miss) will produce more cherries per hour and more hot prospects per hour than any other prospects list you will ever have. By being able to generate more prospects at the top of the temperature gauge in less time, you will improve your revenue and job prospects substantially.

EVEN MORE INFO ON SENDING MATERIAL

The Old Way says, "You mail, you fail." "'Send me something' is an excuse to get you off the phone." Yak yak yak.

I say, "Send me something" means *Send me something!*"

If you are in an industry that relies on personal expertise of the salesperson (adviser), you will note that several of the lead development messages would have you send a résumé. If you sell investments, insurance, real estate, consulting services, or any other product or service requiring special licensing or training, you should have a résumé outlining your qualifications to do the job. If there is any chance that your qualifications may figure into a buying decision, you should even consider having a personal brochure. I have included a résumé template in the download section for this chapter.

USING LEAD DEVELOPMENT MESSAGES

I have thirty or so lead development messages for you. I am not going to go over them all here. I just want to make sure you understand why there are so many.

The best way to show you is just to look at the messages for one lead category, red cherry. Please note: When you see a message with the suffix "email" at the end of its name, this message is identical to the one without this suffix. It has just been formatted to make it easier for you to use as an electronic version. Here's a table explaining what they are:

Message Name	Info Sent
New Red Cherry	Requested info + company info
New Red Cherry Email	Requested info in electronic form + company info
Upgrade to Red Cherry	Requested info
Upgrade to Red Cherry Email	Requested info in electronic form
Downgrade from Hot to Red Cherry	Requested info
Downgrade from Hot to Red Cherry Email	Requested info in electronic form

Let's take an example:

You have a hot prospect. The appointment is set. The lead developer calls to confirm. The prospect says, "Before we go ahead with an appointment, could you send me a few more references to call?"

The "New Red Cherry" letter won't work. Read it.

Dear [Salutation]:

Thanks for taking a moment to visit with me.

I am enclosing the information you requested as well as a little bit about who we are and the kind of business we do.

To make it easier for you to digest this material, I have highlighted some passages for you.

I'll check back in a week to see if you have any questions. If anything comes up earlier, call me at 555-4444.

> *Best regards,*
> *[First name, last name]*
> *[Title]*

That one does not work, does it? But I have one that will, the "Downgrade from Hot to Red Cherry" letter.

Dear [Salutation]:

Thanks for taking the time to visit with me.

I am enclosing the information you requested.

I will be calling you back in about a week. As you look over the material, you might jot down any questions. We can go over your questions when I call.

Moreover, I'll have some questions for you just to make certain that this is right for you at this particular time.

If something comes up earlier, call me at 555-4444.

> *Best regards,*
> *[First name, last name]*
> *[Title]*

The point: when lead type changes, make certain your message exactly fits.

ASSIGNMENT

Download the lead development messages from the chapter 24 download page. The password is justin. (He's my very talented oldest grandson.) Edit as needed. Insert the correct merge fields in each so you can easily merge to a letter, fax, or email from your database. Print the table on pages 1 and 2 to use as a cheat sheet.

25

The Sales Profile

We have two ears and one mouth so we may listen twice as much as we speak.
—Epictetus,
Roman (Greek-born) slave and Stoic philosopher
(AD 55–135)

Now you may think this was not one of my famous statements, and you would, of course, be wrong. You see, in a previous life, I was Epictetus.

With proper credit now accepted, let me state for the record (mine) that I have listened to thousands of sales calls over the years. Based on that, I have concluded that salespeople have twelve mouths and half of an ear.

I am also convinced that an excellent sales questionnaire, which I will refer to as a profile, is the single best tool to ensure that you listen far more than you talk. A profile is also your most powerful lead development and sales tool. As you will learn, your written sales profile has many other benefits as well.

You need to buy Harvey Mackay's book *How to Swim with the Sharks without Being Eaten Alive.*

But don't just buy it; study it, especially Lessons 3, 4, and 5.

In Lesson 3 Mackay writes, "Knowing your customer means knowing what your customer really wants. Maybe it is your product, but maybe there's something else, too: recognition, respect, reliability, concern, service, a feeling of self-importance, friendship, help—things that we all care more about as human beings than we care about malls or envelopes." (Harvey Mackay owns a big envelope manufacturing company.)

In Lesson 4 you'll meet his famous questionnaire, the Mackay 66. It is a sixty-six-question profile, and salespeople at Mackay's envelope company are required to fill it out. It was the most complete questionnaire available—until now, when you take the information in this chapter and craft your own tailored sales profile.

In Lesson 5 Mackay tells war stories on how some very personal questions, not related to business at all, do in fact produce sales.

On our web resources page (your personal password is required) we've posted a link to his website, where you can get a copy of the Mackay 66. Download that now. As you build your profile, you will certainly want to add some or even all of the questions from his "66" to yours.

WHAT IS A PROFILE?

Per Encarta Online, a profile is "a brief description that summarizes the characteristics of somebody or something."

Someone is old or young, a boss or an employee, rich or poor, better or worse. They are married, divorced, separated, or single. They are fathers, daughters, husbands, wives. The fabric of our lives is a crazy quilt of color and cloth, with countless thousands of threads stitching the pieces together to produce the characteristics that are uniquely each of us.

Therefore the questions you ask to know your customer must mirror the complexity of that life.

A sales profile, then, would be the questions you ask and the answers you receive to those questions as well as any observations you make. It's certainly not enough to have your client fill out a questionnaire and to think you now have a profile. Much of the magic in profiling comes from observing the responses to your questions.

As you study the Mackay 66, you cannot miss the fact that many of his questions have nothing to do with business. You would think, as the owner of an envelope company, that his questions would include:

How big?
How many?
What color?
Which paper?

There is not a single one of those questions on his profile.

Instead, he wants to know spouse's education, anniversary, and military service. They are mostly about the person, not the company.

Why are questions like this so important?

I will let Mr. Mackay answer:

"[Buyers] . . . come prewired to regard your proposition with suspicion and cynicism. That's their job.

"It's your job as a salesperson to neutralize these feelings so your product can get the fair hearing it deserves."

To this I would add: it's your job to create an almost unbreakable bond by understanding your prospective or current client better than anyone else.

People buy for many reasons. It's your job to explore all the attributes as early in the relationship as possible so you will understand this client as no one has before.

Questions are the answer.

Let's now get into the nitty-gritty (mine) of profile design.

HOW LONG SHOULD A PROFILE BE?

Harvey Mackay obviously answered this question: it should be long, at least sixty-six questions.

My answer: a single profile should be relatively short but have lots of microprofiles. On complicated and very personal products, such as financial services, you could have 20 or 30 profiles with, perhaps, a total of 150 questions.

But clients won't sit still and answer 100 or more questions! Will they?

In one sitting? No.

Here's how it works:

First, you will have several profiles. They have different purposes, and may be asked over a series of phone calls and meetings, perhaps over a period as long as a year. Don't worry, this doesn't mean you have to wait a year for a sale. Over that year you will be strengthening your relationship.

Two of your profiles are:

1. *Preliminary qualification.* These are your basic "interest, money, and time" questions. They are asked very early on the first contact. The lead developer owns this profile.

2. *Status quo.* This profile will determine if you and your prospect are a good fit. The lead developer normally owns this questionnaire also, but in the case of a hot prospect who sets up an appointment quickly, the salesperson should still go through its most important questions.

We will cover the other profiles momentarily.

Part of the lead development process, as you learn in subsequent chapters, is *answering questions.* A prospect who doesn't ask questions will not buy. But it is the lead developer and the salesperson asking questions that ultimately cause the prospects to ask *their* own questions. The prospect starting to ask questions is the best signal that now is the time to set up the appointment for the salesperson. When the prospect starts asking the salesperson questions is the signal that it's *very nearly* the time to close the sale. (More to follow in chapter 26, "Client and Prospect Education," on question answering.)

Let's suppose that you are a lead developer. You aren't sure what to say on your next call. If in doubt, ask some questions from one or more of your profiles. As you express interest in your prospect, by listening far more than you talk, you will find what the prospect wants and fears, and you will build that almost magical bond. When that has occurred, the prospect will slide easily over into the selling cycle.

A lead developer continues asking as many questions about the product, the buying process, and the status quo until the prospect starts asking questions back. Then you most likely have a hot one.

Should Your Sales Questionnaire Be Written?

This is almost a stupid question.

Of course it should.

But most are not.

When I conduct a seminar, I frequently ask, "How many of you do an in-depth profile of a prospective client?" Most hands go up. Then I say, "If you use a written sales profile, leave your hand up." Most hands go down.

Here is an equally dumb question:

Why should a sales questionnaire be written?

It is more professional.

People are used to giving true answers to a written questionnaire. Consider a visit to the doctor. You first check in where they qualify you (Who is your insurance carrier?). Then they give you a questionnaire; it's generally a tenth-generation photocopy. You fill it out, answering all kinds of questions about the vile and loathsome diseases that have affected you and your family members. You calmly write down the family history of insanity. You then give this questionnaire to a complete stranger and go into a room, take off all your clothes, and sit on a cold metal table. That is the power of a written questionnaire! And the real profile (the exam) has not even begun!

You won't forget the important questions, which means you will get answers instead of the nothing you get to a question you forgot to ask.

When you commit it to writing, you can now improve it.

Perhaps most important, a finely honed written questionnaire will help you find the two basic reasons why someone will change what they may have been doing for a lifetime and instead do what you want them to do.

The two basic reasons, of course, are: (1) help them achieve a positive goal they have not yet attained; and (2) help them reduce or eliminate a current or potential threat.

When you find both the positives and the negatives, you can frequently move even the most stubborn prospect. A well-designed questionnaire that finds what they want and what they fear will pop them loose almost every time.

Here's an additional reason why the questionnaire should be written: because the boss says so. It's a discipline. Harvey Mackay enforced it at Mackay Envelope. Based on my complete overhaul of our questionnaire process, you can depend on the fact that our questionnaire process is now in place and enforced.

FINDING GOOD QUESTIONS

I have long felt that the best sources of good questions are top-producing salespeople. Those who have made it to the top of the food chain *always* have a written or minimally a mental library of questions they use to get to know the customer.

I'm sure Mr. Mackay's questions came from his own experience in the field. From reading his book, you will see he is not just an armchair executive making stuff up. He's been in there slugging it out with the rest of the workforce.

As Bill Good Marketing's chief salesman, I designed the questionnaires we use in our sales process. In many of my own sales interviews,

I try out new questions. If they create an impact, I may add them to our own written questionnaire.

Whenever I design questionnaires for salespeople in other industries, I don't just make stuff up. I get people in the field to tell me which questions work best. I then take the best of those questions, apply some principles of questionnaire design, and more often than not, I create a winner.

My first effort at this was about ten years ago when I called several of my most successful clients in the financial services industry. Each was making more than $1 million a year. I simply asked them, "What are your favorite questions to ask prospects or clients?"

From those questions I built what I called the million-dollar questionnaire.

I'd been pretty happy with this questionnaire and haven't felt a particular need to update it. Was I in for a surprise when I decided to take it back to the drawing board! (Mine.)

You see, I have a resource most writers on sales don't have. I write for one of the major trade magazines in the financial services industry, *Research* magazine, and over the years I have periodically made my readers offers they couldn't refuse.

Some years ago I told them, "Send me your best closing question and I'll send you the best of the best." On another occasion, "Send me a copy of your sales proposal and I'll send you an individual critique." (To deliver on my end, I had to write 101 personal letters, but I found out for certain how skilled the advisers in my industry were with proposal writing. Only 2 of the 101 proposals I received were up to professional grade.)

To do further research on profiling I asked my readers, "Send me your three best profiling questions and I'll send you the complete list."

I received more than 770 questions, and as I write this, we are still counting.

I had all the questions copied to an Excel spreadsheet. Then the fun started. I took each question, one at a time, and assigned each to a category. As I studied and revised the categories, I realized I had identified the primary attributes of a financial planning client.

After a lot of study, I weeded these down to twenty-four attributes. What would an attribute be?

Back to Encarta. An attribute is "a feature or distinctive part of something."

According to me, "If you understand the attributes, you understand the whole." (Possibly a future famous statement.)

And in your industry, there are also twenty-four attributes, more or less.

In the table that follows, I have defined each of the attributes that some of the best salespeople in the world are striving to discover. A few of these obviously apply only to financial services, but most apply to any product. (Remember, MacKay sells envelopes. The MacKay 66 includes nothing about them.)

I've also included sample questions these top salespeople asked to discover these attributes.

So even if you are selling deodorant or cream for dry and flaky horse hooves, all twenty-four (more or less) attributes may apply.

My reason for including questions peculiar to the financial services industry is that by studying them, you may be reminded of a similar attribute in your own prospects and clients.

ASSIGNMENT

First study the attributes, their definitions, and the following sample questions.

Then log on to our website and download this table in Microsoft Word. Add your own questions. Make up as many as you can. Better to have too many than too few.

The password is jasonmatthew. (Jason and Matthew are my nephews, wonderful boys who grew up to be wonderful men.)

Attribute	Attribute Defined	Sample Questions
Business background	What the person does or did for a living.	How did you get started in this job? How long have you worked for [company]? What do you see as the biggest challenge to your industry (profession, job, career, etc.)?

Attribute	Attribute Defined	Sample Questions
Business competition	Assesses the strengths and weaknesses of the competitors. Find out what you must and must not do to succeed in this relationship.	Are you committed to any of these holdings, or to any of your current advisers? What do you like about working with your current investment professional? If you could, what would you improve?
Buying process	The way in which a person or individual makes buying decisions.	What have been your previous sources for investment knowledge? What is your process/discipline for making investment decisions?
Customer expectations	What the client expects (and is expected to do). Expectations can fall into at least five subcategories: 1. Product 2. Salesperson 3. Company 4. Economy 5. What the company expects of the client.	Do you think inflation or taxes will go up or down in the next ten years? We seek to be the primary source of investment advice for our clients. What must we as a team do to gain your respect and trust as financial professionals? What could we as a company do that would cause us to lose your business?

Attribute	Attribute Defined	Sample Questions
Customer and you	Defines potential barriers and issues between salesperson and customer. This covers some of the questions from Mackay's "The Customer and You" section. "Does the proposal you plan to make to him/her require the customer to change a habit or take an action that is contrary to custom?" *	How would you describe the perfect client/adviser relationship you are searching for?
Fear	Barriers, fears the client must overcome to achieve goals and peace of mind.	Are you highly confident that your retirement income will be sufficient to support your current lifestyle, or do you have concerns that at some point during your retirement you might run out of money? What are you doing now with your investments that makes you most uncomfortable?

* This question is taken verbatim from the Mackay 66.

Attribute	Attribute Defined	Sample Questions
Financial legacy	Really a subcategory of risk management regarding intentions to leave a legacy.	If you could create a charitable foundation, what cause would it support? If you could leave a legacy, who would be beneficiary?
Financial risk management	How the client manages the usual risks to life and loss of income.	Has there been a recent birth or death in your family or extended family? How did you determine the amount of life insurance you now carry?
Financial risk tolerance	Estimate the client's tolerance for risk.	Are you willing to lose larger sums of money in the short term to enjoy potentially higher returns longer term?
General family	Captures a snapshot of the family relations and obligations.	Is there anyone else in your life you may have a future financial responsibility for? Your parents are all set? The in-laws? How many children? What are their ages?

Attribute	Attribute Defined	Sample Questions
Important family information	Important dates and other information that anyone contacting this person should know. Use this to build goodwill.	When did you get married? Your birth date is? Kids' birth dates? Spouse's birth date?
Personal education	Covers both education and military service.	How important was your education in helping you get where you are today? Where did you graduate from [high school, college]?
Personal goals	A specific state of affairs a person is trying to achieve.	If you were given a briefcase with _____ dollars, what would you do with it? When do you plan to retire?
Personal history	Background; helpful in understanding current situation.	What person had the greatest impact in shaping your life? How? Where did you grow up?
Personal lifestyle	How the buyer lives.	What is your favorite pastime or hobby? What is a "great day"?

Attribute	Attribute Defined	Sample Questions
Personal special interests	Looking for passions, what they really like to do.	What do you do for fun? What kind of pets do you and your family have?
Personal values	The ideals, principles, or beliefs that a person finds worthwhile or desirable.	What is the thing in your life that makes you happiest right now? What provides meaningful purpose in your life?
Personal vision	Questions to elicit how the client sees life in the future. In my opinion, probably the highest expression of what a person wants.	If you could tear up your day planner and set up your week however you wanted, what would that look like? If you won the lottery, what would you do?
Planning	Ideas on how to achieve their goals.	Why do you feel that planning is important to your future financial success? Do you have a written plan designed to meet your goals?

Attribute	Attribute Defined	Sample Questions
Product expertise	Extent of client knowledge about your product or service.	What types of investments are you familiar with? Do you find when it comes to making an investment decision that you almost always know exactly what to do?
Product strategy (investment strategy for financial services)	How the client intends to attain the benefit offered by your product or service.	Do you have an investment strategy and philosophy? Do you consider yourself in the wealth preservation or the wealth accumulation stage of your life?
Set the stage	Questions to get the client or prospect answering questions.	I have a lot of questions I'd like to ask you, but before we get started, is there anything that you're concerned about that you want to make sure we cover today? What were you hoping to accomplish today?

Attribute	Attribute Defined	Sample Questions
Status quo—business	These questions give you a picture of the scope of a business or department. In our Profiles, we create a one-page sheet for this info called something like "business profile."	Ballpark, how much are you spending a year on advertising? You've been in your present position how long?
Status quo—product	Questions to determine how the prospect uses type of product now. Status quo questions look for missing benefits and dissatisfaction.	How has the volatility in the market affected your feelings about investments over the past few months? I Iow satisfied are you now with your financial situation?

DEVELOPING THE PROFILE

To have a good profile, you need a lot of questions. Hopefully you came up with at least five questions for each of the attributes above. If not, do not pass Go. Go back and do it.

To help you develop a profile, let's prepare a case study, a method of learning about a complex process by examining in detail a single instance.

The complex process, in this case, is profile design.

The instance of it is the profile I will design for my own company based on the principles I developed while analyzing the more than 770 questions I received from my *Research* magazine readers.

To learn how to develop your own profile, first read the pages that follow as I take you through the process of upgrading the profiles we use at my company. This is the case study. By then you should have the idea of how to do it. I will give you some additional help in an online document, "Sales Profile."

Where to Start

You may start with any attribute. However, the attribute I chose to start with is status quo.

Per Encarta Online, *status quo* is "the condition or state of affairs that currently exists."

But let's further define it: By status quo, I mean the existing state of affairs your prospect experiences without your product or service or with a competitor's product. If you know the status quo, you have a starting point to determine the extent to which your prospect needs your product or service. If you sell armadillo burgers, your status quo profile would find out who your prospect's customers are, what other kind of specialty burgers might be served, how well they sell, and how happy the customers are with them.

Once you understand your prospect's status quo, you can understand how your product fills the prospect's needs. As you ask questions about the benefits that your product has that your prospect does not enjoy, watch as the interest level ratchets up.

DEVELOPING QUESTIONS
FOR THE STATUS QUO ATTRIBUTE

1. Define the primary benefits your product or service offers.
2. Build questions around those benefits to see whether your prospective client has these benefits, needs them, or even wants them.

To do this effectively, I first developed a simple worksheet for this attribute. You will find the worksheet in the download section of this chapter. You already have the password.

Here's the worksheet with my answers provided. You can obviously develop several questions from one benefit.

Define the primary product you sell. The Bill Good Marketing System is a computer-based, client-marketing, prospecting, and office-management system.

Define the benefits of each part of the definition and then write questions to determine if the client has or needs these benefits.

Computer-Based

Benefit: Easily sends letters, faxes, and emails.

Question: Which program are you using for your database management?

Question: Are you able to send letters, faxes, and emails while making sure that your clients and prospects get their messages in the manner they prefer?

Benefit: A cohesive system ensures that important information, such as sales opportunities are never missed, because these opportunities are periodically reviewed.

Question: What kind of reporting do you have to ensure that you don't ever forget a sales opportunity?

Benefit: Multimedia training is available so that people operating the program are trained in the same way the last person was trained, which means there is continuity in the way data are entered and updated.

Question: Who is primarily responsible for ensuring that data are entered correctly, the system is backed up, and a separate backup is taken off-site at least once a week?

Question: When you bring on a new team member, how is he or she trained on your database?

Benefit: Specifically designed for a team so that the person in charge can easily see that team members are doing what they are supposed to do.

Question: How do you use [name of program] to monitor whether your team is doing what they are supposed to do?

Client Marketing

Benefit: Improve client retention.

Question: What is your client retention strategy?

Benefit: Generate business now.

Question: How do you use client marketing to generate business now?

Benefit: Develop business for the future.

Question: What kind of campaigns do you run to make certain that you know of any future business opportunities with your clients?

Prospecting

Benefit: A unique strategy designed to promote, not solicit referrals.

Question: What is your strategy to generate more referrals?

Question: How do you feel about asking for referrals? Do you like doing that?

Benefit: System in place designed to develop and manage strategic partners.

Question: Do you refer business to other related professionals but do not receive an equivalent referral business back to you?

Question: What are some of the categories of related professionals that you should pursue but have not?

Benefit: Two different methods to "clone your best clients," meaning, develop more clients just like the good ones you have now.

Question: What does the phrase "clone your best clients" mean to you?

Question: What are you doing to find more clients exactly like your best ones?

Benefit: We have a "new identity" campaign to help develop a professional identity with people you know by cultivating a business contact into a client.

Question: Our surveys show that after referrals, the most popular choice in developing new clients is networking. Do you network at all? If yes: Do you network mostly with social or business contacts? If no: We may have an easy way for you to get started. Let me ask you a couple of more questions.

Question: How many people would you say you know through a business affiliation that you would like to do business with but have found it awkward to approach?

Benefit: We have a campaign designed to develop your social connections—the people you know and would like to do business with, but cannot solicit because to do so would be a social error of the first order.

Question: How many people do you know socially you would like to do business with but can't solicit their business directly because it would be socially unacceptable to do so?

Office Management

Benefit: Create a team structure to perform the nonsales functions so the sales professional spends all or most of his time selling.

Question: What do you have in the way of staff support?

Question: Do you know how to go about building a team?

Benefit: Our system provides organizational processes for recurring events and actions.

Question: How organized are you?

Question: What's your process when you get a referral?

Question: What's your process to confirm an appointment?

Benefit: Reduce time spent in service.

Question: What percentage of your time do you spend servicing your clients?

VISIONS/VALUES/GOALS/FEARS

As already stated, people will make a fundamental change for two reasons:

They will make a fundamental change in order to achieve one or more positive goals, generally something they have wanted for some time. If you show them how to do this, and if they realistically believe that your product or service will assist them to attain their goals, they will do whatever it takes to buy your product. If your product or service will help people achieve more than one goal, the probability of getting the sale is that much higher.

Someone will also buy your product if it helps them avoid something they do not want but have, something they hate but that affects them, and especially some condition now, or projected into the future, that they fear.

You sell best if you know the positives and the negatives.

If you designed your status quo per my recommendations, you will discover many things about your product and service that people want, and you will likely discover some conditions in their business or life that they don't like, they hate, or even that they fear.

But what if you could tie your product to parts of their lives other than business? People buy things for all kinds of reasons. If you understand people better by knowing where they are going, what they see of the future, and what in particular they are trying to accomplish, your relationship will be tighter, which in turn helps to make additional sales as well as fend off competitors. This is what Harvey Mackay talked about in his book.

To get this information, add a profile or four of them. You could call it simply "Goals." It should explore these four attributes:

Visions: Where they want to go in the future.

Values: The ideals, principles, or beliefs that a person finds worthwhile or desirable.

Understanding a person's values will tell you if this is someone you want to develop a long-term relationship with. Remember, one purpose of a profile is to find out if you want this person, not just to get them to want you. It has to be a two-way street. (Mine, age seven.)

Goals: Specific, measurable accomplishments. "I want to be promoted to senior vice president by my forty-fifth birthday." This is a goal.

Fear: This is where you probably will find the negatives that can be powerful motivators. I would certainly not use "Fear" as a title of a profile that the prospect might see. I would use something like "Change and Obstacles" or "Challenges to Overcome."

BUILDING YOUR GOALS PROFILE

I am going to make this easy for you. I went through my question library on these attributes and crafted a goals profile for my company. I consider these fairly generic questions, appropriate to any selling situation. If you are in financial services, I have provided additional questions for you on the website in the download section for this chapter. In the same section I also have provided this profile in Microsoft Word format. You can use this as a model and adapt it as needed.

Vision Questions

If you won the lottery, what would you do?

Where do you see yourself in five years?

What do you see yourself doing ten years from now? Twenty years?

If you had all the money you needed, what would you do differently in life?

What has to happen in your life for you to consider yourself truly successful?

If you could be doing anything else right now, what would it be?
Imagine your best day ever. What are you doing?
What could impact your future right now?

Values Questions

What do you consider your primary obligation as a [business owner, parent, husband/wife/life partner]?

What is the most important thing in your life?

Why do you work?

Why would you retire?

What things in your life do you consider more important than money?

Goals

What three things have you not yet done in your life, but are determined to do? Travel? Start a business? Sail around the world?

What are you trying to accomplish?

Is there anything that you're doing now that in four years you don't want to be doing? Is there anything you're not doing now that you would like to be doing?

What major purchases will you be making in the near future?

What are you hoping your money will accomplish for you?

Fear

What is holding you back from reaching your personal financial goals?

What is the biggest concern you have currently?

What are you most afraid of losing?

ASSIGNMENT

Your assignment is to develop your own profile. In the download section for this chapter you will find help on the other attributes plus various worksheets and samples.

A note of caution: it should take some hours of thought to do this. Thinking is good.

26

Client and Prospect Education

In following up on red cherries, green cherries, and info leads, the lead developer will discover many problems and opportunities requiring education. Most of the education should be done by the salesperson, but the lead developer directs the prospect to the educational material on your website and sends white papers, DVDs, and MP3 files.

The entire purpose of client and prospect education is to increase the desire to own the benefits of your product or service by showing the client how your product or service helps them achieve the positive and avoid or reduce the negative.

At the risk of being too repetitious, let's redefine our terms:

Feature: A prominent aspect of something. (One of the features of the new house is that its walls are made from material optimized to transmit wireless signals.)

Benefit: An advantage, help, or aid. (Building materials that have been optimized for wireless transmission means that your TV and Internet signals will be crisp and clear.) I made up electronically optimized building materials. But it sounds like it would sell if there could be any such thing.

DESIGNING AN EDUCATIONAL PRESENTATION

Even a simple product like armadillo burgers could generate reams of educational material. You could go on and on about low-fat advantage, about the use of their natural oils in cooking, and about how armadillos are pests destroying the groundhog population. Out of all of this information, what does your prospect need to know?

To answer my own question, let me remind you that people buy benefits but they will ask questions about features. When you buy a new car, you are buying look, style, image, and safety, but you ask questions about steering, brakes, gas mileage, and the like.

We want them asking questions. Questions are a sign of interest.

Therefore, educate your prospects on the benefits of your product and provide only bare-bones info on product features until *asked*.

A note of caution: Teaching people to prepare a correct educational presentation is tough. Listen to countless salespeople, as I have, and you'll discover that most of them drone on about features. People's eyes glaze over.

Probably the best way to learn is for a lead developer to listen to a skilled salesperson, keeping his or her mouth shut. Very early in your training, your sales manager should monitor your phone calls. He or she also should be able to send you instant messages directing specifically what to say or not.

A new armadillo burger salesman who has steered off into how armadillo hunting will restore the groundhog population might get this IM: "Explain 'Low-fat benefit.'"

Other IMs could be:

"Listen."

"He didn't answer question. Repeat it."

"Close for two cases of burgers."

Let's look at some examples. First we'll look at a script focusing on a feature, and we'll look at another focusing only on benefits, entirely omitting the feature.

FEATURE-FOCUSED SCRIPT

I will just use a product I know. Suppose I am explaining a particular feature called title logic, which is used in the Bill Good Marketing software. I could say:

"One of the features of the Bill Good Marketing System software is called title logic. It's basically some programming that takes information about the client in your database and figures out the best way to address a letter."

You really need that, right?

BENEFIT-FOCUSED SCRIPT

See if this makes you a little more interested.

"One of the things about our software that you will enjoy is certainty that all of your cards and letters are correctly addressed.

"This might not sound like much, but suppose for a second you are going to send a letter to Dr. Joe Blow, M.D. He paid $500,000 for those two letters after his name, and he knows that the correct way to address an M.D. is, Joe Blow, M.D., not Dr. Joe Blow, M.D. Real doctors don't use Dr. and M.D. The software takes care of this automatically for you."

PROSPECT: How does it do that?
YOU: It's a feature of the program called "Title Logic."

METHODS TO EDUCATE

There are several ways to skin the client educational cat. (You have to check my earlier book, *Prospecting Your Way to Sales Success,* for the etymology of "more than one way to skin a cat.")

Most often you simply explain how a particular feature works, focusing on the benefits of the feature as opposed to the feature itself.

You can send a white paper.

When I Googled "white paper," I found 88 million hits. You can even get a white paper on how to write a white paper.

We have white papers on virtually every aspect of our system. At the drop of a hat (mine), we will send one.

Other companies do this as well. We just copied the format Microsoft has on its website. If it works for them . . . For your convenience, I've put a copy of our white paper template in the downloads section for this chapter. The password is lucas. (My middle grandson.)

A major benefit of a white paper is that you don't have to spend a lot of money on expensive color printing and then throw out half of it when the pricing, product features, or something else changes.

Online Resources

One of the most valuable online resources is an online conference service, which enables you to give a slide-show presentation and record it, complete with questions and answers. Then you can post it to the web.

This can be a major time-saver, especially when you have multiple people on a buying committee. The salesperson might spend an hour on such a presentation only to learn that there is another decision-maker. So the lead developer could chase up the other team members and get them to listen to the presentation.

I keep an up-to-date list of the web conference services we recommend on our web resources page, which is available through your personal password.

You also can post white papers, brochures, and MP3 files of happy customers singing your praises.

The Sale Begins When . . .

One of the great old sales trainers, Elmer Leterman, wrote a book called *The Sale Begins When the Customer Says "No."**

This, of course, is a supreme statement of what I have characterized as the Old Way. The sale does not begin when the customer says no. It begins when the customer is interested enough to seriously consider buying your product.

This brings us to closing signals.

How do you know if the prospect is interested enough to be moved into a selling cycle?

The simple answer is, unless you've blown it by talking too much, the prospect will begin asking pointed questions. These questions will tend to focus on how something works, whether it has this or that feature, and so on.

This particular question-asking behavior can begin anywhere, but most often it begins after a series of questions from one or more of your profiles.

When the lead developer hears these questions, it's time to say, "You know, you're getting a little bit above my pay grade. I would like you to talk to my partner."

Most salespeople—especially new kids on the block—talk way too much. They tend to answer all possible questions a prospect could ask. If there are no commonsense questions remaining, obviously the prospect can't ask. And you have thereby destroyed the best signal you

---

* Now out of print, this book was published by Greenberg Publishing Company.

will ever receive, the one that tells you it's time to move this into the selling phase.

A similar behavior can be noted when it's time to close the sale. Assuming you have left open some key areas the prospect can ask questions about, there is a point at which the prospect will take control of the selling cycle and ask a series of questions, mostly about product features.

The only way I know to teach the ability to recognize this signal is for an experienced sales manager to monitor the calls of a rookie, and the instant that blabbermouthing is detected, scribble a note, make a gesture, or send an instant message. (Instant messaging is the best way to coach a new lead developer or even a veteran salesperson. Sales managers should be frequently listening in on calls, and when your salesperson steers off the true path, ding 'em with an IM.)

THE LEAD DEVELOPER'S JOB

The lead developer's job is to stay in touch with red cherries, green cherries, info leads, and pitch-and-misses.

He or she answers questions, provides additional information, continues getting more questions from the profile answered, and when that magic moment comes, smoothly moves the prospect over to the salesperson by setting up an appointment or by transferring the call right then.

That's lead development.

27

Case Study

Developing a Lead

Let's say you sell advertising for a company that provides direct-mail advertising for home improvement companies. They create four-color postcards and send them in decks to hundreds of thousands of home owners. (Okay, okay. In the interest of full disclosure, my son-in-law Devin owns part of the Oregon franchise for RSVP Marketing.) Nevertheless, it's a good example. So follow along.

Let's assume that the CEO of RSVP, Bob Lippmann, is doing what I recommend and personally testing what he wants his staff to be doing. One day he takes an incoming call from a prospect who owns a company that installs electronic fences—the kind that keeps the dogs in the yard by giving them a zap when they get too close to the boundary. He has received your latest card deck from RSVP at home and calls the office.

BOB: Good morning. RSVP Marketing. This is Bob. How can we help you?

PROSPECT: I got your postcard deck at home, and I was wondering about your prices and whether this is something I should consider advertising with.

BOB: Very possibly. By the way, who am I speaking with?

PROSPECT: My name is Qui T. Barkin. My company is Zap Your Dog.

BOB [taking out his basic qualification questionnaire]: Mr. Barkin, we probably can help you, but let me check a couple of questions with you first. What exactly do you do at Zap Your Dog?

PROSPECT: We make an electronic fence for keeping dogs on the property without having to put up one of those vinyl fences.

(This is a type of business you deal with.)

BOB: You are located where?
PROSPECT: West Portland.

(He's in your area.)

BOB: And over how wide an area do you market?
PROSPECT: Most of our business is in the Portland area.

(Excellent. He could go in several different card decks.)

BOB: You've been in business since when?
PROSPECT: 1993.

(They've been around long enough to pay their bills.)

BOB: In terms of capacity, how many new clients could you deal with in a month?
PROSPECT: About eighty.

(They are big enough to not get completely overwhelmed by a lot of new leads.)

BOB: How many new clients are you getting now?
PROSPECT: We are handling about sixty new customers a month.

(Definite need for our service.)

BOB: Depending on a number of factors, we could design an advertising program for you for $5,000 to $25,000. If you liked the results other companies in the home improvement industry have enjoyed, would an advertising budget in that range be feasible?
PROSPECT: Yes, we could do that.

(He has the interest, has the money, and can make the decision. Let's see if we have a hot prospect.)

BOB: I would like to set up a time for my senior account executive, Devin Stokes, owner of our Oregon division, to come visit your shop, get a good understanding of your products and your client base, and then show you how we might help you generate more business. He has an appointment in Multnomah next Tuesday. I have a spot open at 2:00 PM and again at 3:30 PM. Which of those would work better for you?

PROSPECT: Either of those could work, but before we set a time, I'd really like to see some information on what the program is all about and especially on what your company does. There are a lot of people out there selling advertising, and our company has been taken to the cleaners a few times.

If you were an Old Way sales professional, you would immediately respond, "No problem. I'll make certain that Devin brings that information with him. Would two o'clock or three thirty be better?" Fortunately for Mr. Qui T. Barkin, you do not subscribe to that tired old theory, and you are building your sales system on the belief that buyers tend to be truth-tellers. So you proceed as a Good Way practitioner.

BOB: No problem. I'll put this in the mail to you right away. You should receive it tomorrow or the next day. Will you have time to look it over by, say, Thursday [today plus three days]?

PROSPECT: Yes, I could do that.

BOB: Great. I'll give you a call on Thursday. Normally, what's the best time of day to reach you?

PROSPECT: The earlier in the day the better. I usually get here around 8:00 AM.

BOB: Great. I'll call you early Thursday morning. And have a great day.

Okay, we tested the water and found that we do *not* have a hot prospect, so we're going to send him the "New Red Cherry" letter. We'll enclose our corporate brochure because we want to put our best foot forward (mine, remember?) and use it to reduce fear by showing how long we've been around and how stable we are. An electronic copy of the brochure just does not deliver the same impact. Naturally, we also will be implementing the mutilation principle by putting a sticky note on the cover of the brochure telling him "see page 9." (This page focuses on company stability. It includes reference to BBB membership and shows that the company was founded in 1985.)

Where are we with this prospect?

We have a red cherry, not a hot prospect.

This is a prospect who needs our service and can afford it.

What's our plan for the next call?

Unless he's ready to set up an appointment, we will use one or more of our profiles to see if we can find some additional reasons to set up an appointment now. Failing that, we want to keep Mr. Barkin as a red cherry. Failing that, we want to downgrade him no further than a green cherry. Reminder: When we have any subsequent contact with a cherry (red or green) or any other prospect, we never ask if he received the information we sent or even if he read it. That invites yet one more phone call. Again, our prospects are truth-tellers and "doers of what they say they will do."

RECEPTION: Good morning. Zap Your Dog. How can we help you this morning?

BOB: Good morning, this is Bob Lippmann at RSVP Marketing. Who am I speaking with?

RECEPTION: This is Valerie.

BOB: Hi, Valerie. I need to speak with Qui. I promised I would call him early this morning. Is he available?

RECEPTION: One moment, please.

PROSPECT: This is Qui.

BOB: Good morning, Qui. This is Bob Lippmann with RSVP Marketing. We sent you that information on Monday [today minus three days] about our advertising program, but before I recommend you get involved, there are a few questions I would like to check with you. Is now an okay time?

PROSPECT: That would be fine.

BOB [status quo profile is on his desk]: Excellent. Tell me Qui, what are you trying to accomplish with your advertising?

PROSPECT: I need on average twenty more leads a month. What I really mean is I need enough leads to generate twenty more closes a month, which means I need about forty more appointments.

BOB: What is your best source right now?

PROSPECT: After we do an installation, we take a picture of the dog running around the yard, make a flyer, and distribute it several blocks around.

BOB: That's clever. And what is your least successful source?

PROSPECT: Probably newspaper advertising. We feel we have to be in there, but it's just nothing we can count on. Sometimes the phone rings. Sometimes it doesn't.

BOB: Other than flyers and phone books, where do you spend the rest of your advertising dollars?

PROSPECT: We advertise in a magazine that goes to veterinarian offices. Results have been pretty good, but I need to tell you that I just committed our advertising budget for the next quarter to an expanded edition of that magazine. I'm just not going to have more funds available for a while.

(Bummer. Our red cherry prospect has dropped down a notch and is a greenie at best.)

BOB: I understand. Tell me, when will you be considering your next advertising expenditure?

PROSPECT: We do this once a quarter.

BOB: Very good. I'm going to put you down for a callback in three months. For now, I'm going to send you a white paper, "Controlling Lead Flow with RSVP." And from time to time I will send you information about how some of the other home improvement businesses are doing with our program. Since you are on our residential mailing list, be on a lookout for our card deck every month or so. So that we can keep our postage bill down and perhaps save some trees, may I have your email address with the understanding that if you don't want me to use email, I won't?

PROSPECT: Email is fine. My address is qui.t.barkin@zapyour dog.com.

BOB: Great. We will stay in touch, and I hope that the new advertising works for you. Thankyouverymuch. [Click. Dial tone.]

We need to send Qui a message. Remember, every time there is a change in lead status, we use that as an excuse to send a message. Since he dropped from a new red cherry to a green cherry, we'll send him an email, "Downgrade to Green Cherry Email." We'll add a postscript as follows:

"PS: As promised, I am sending you our white paper 'Controlling Lead Flow with RSVP.' I think you will especially enjoy page 4."

Between now and three months from now, your objective is to stay on his mental shelf. If you disappear from view, when you call back in three months you'll have to start all over. With a prospect that could be a $25,000-a-year client, I would have him on a forty-five-day call so he hears from you at least once before you call for an appointment in three months. Your phone contact can be a voice-mail message.

The saga continues forty-five days later:

RECEPTION: Good morning. Zap Your Dog. How can we help you?

BOB: Good morning. Is this Valerie?

RECEPTION: Yes, it is.

BOB: Good morning, Valerie. This is Bob at RSVP Marketing. I need to leave Qui a voice mail message. Could you transfer me?

RECEPTION: Certainly, Bob.

PROSPECT'S VOICE MAIL: This is Qui T. Barkin. Leave a message.

BOB: Good morning, Qui. Bob Lippmann at RSVP Marketing. We're the company that does direct-mail advertising to high-end homeowners here in Portland. We spoke about six weeks ago. I'll be calling you, as we agreed, in about another six weeks. In the meantime, I wanted to suggest you visit our website. We've just posted some new testimonials there. If you have a minute or two, drop by www.rsvpmarketing.com. Have a great day, and if you have any questions, you can always call me at 1-800-994-7787.

Six weeks later:

RECEPTION: Good morning. Zap Your Dog. How can we help you?

BOB: Good morning, Valerie. This is Bob with RSVP Marketing. I promised Qui I would get back with him. Could you connect me, please?

RECEPTION: One moment, please.

PROSPECT: Qui here.

BOB: Good morning, Qui. This is Bob Lippmann with RSVP Marketing. We spoke three months ago about our direct-mail advertising program. We agreed we would get back in touch about now. What I would like to do first, if that's okay, is review our last call and then check over a few more questions. Do you have just a few minutes for me right now?

PROSPECT: I'm busy, but I can spare five minutes.

BOB: Thanks. You told me we needed about forty new leads a month to get you the twenty additional sales you needed, correct?

PROSPECT: Yes. And that's still pretty much the case.

BOB: So your magazine didn't deliver, correct?

PROSPECT: Some, but not what we wanted.

BOB: Getting those additional forty leads a month is still very important to you, correct?

PROSPECT: It's my top priority.

BOB: Is your advertising budget still open for the next quarter?

PROSPECT: I have not committed it yet. I've actually been waiting to see if you would call.

(Sounds smokin' hot to me. Let's find out.)

BOB: Well, I think we have an excellent chance to help you hit the target you've set. My boss, Devin Stokes, has a couple of open spots this week. He could see you at 8:00 AM on Tuesday or at 8:30 AM on Friday morning. Which of those looks better for you?

PROSPECT: Let's do it Friday morning.

BOB: Great. I'll confirm that by email today. Then we'll call your office on Thursday just to make certain nothing came up. Who should we talk to?

PROSPECT: Valerie is the one. She knows my schedule.

BOB: Very good. Devin will see you Friday morning.

You have a hot prospect. We'll send our "hot out-of-office appointment" email. Also, we'll schedule a telephone confirmation the day before. The lead developer would normally do this call.

THE FIRST APPOINTMENT

When Devin picks up his appointment folders for Friday, the profiles should be right on top. He studies them and decides to complete the company profile and ask additional questions from the personal and family dynamics profile. Remember, the profiles are rarely filled out in a single session.

Very important note: A salesperson will *always* need to give some explanation as to why some fairly personal questions are being asked.

The prospect must agree to provide answers. Otherwise the conversation will be extremely awkward.

Examples:

DEVIN: Qui, before we get into the specifics of our advertising program, I really want to find out about you. We've found over the years that there are several possible areas we can misjudge and therefore make recommendations that miss the mark. We can miss if we don't understand how your business develops and processes leads. We can miss if we don't understand your business objectives. And we can miss if we don't understand some things about you and your role here at Zap Your Dog. The only way I know to understand the whole is by understanding the parts, and we get there by asking a lot of questions. May I run a few personal questions by you?

PROSPECT: Sure.

DEVIN: Excellent. On a bit of a personal note, are you married?

PROSPECT: Fifteen years now.

DEVIN: Her name is . . .

PROSPECT: Noelle. We call her "No" for short.

(Uh-oh.)

DEVIN: To what extent is she involved in the business?

PROSPECT: She keeps our books and signs the checks.

(Uh-oh. Another decision-maker.)

DEVIN [from the expectations questionnaire]: What's the process here at Zap Your Dog for spending money on advertising, new equipment, stuff like that?

(Questions do not have to be asked in order but they can be.)

PROSPECT: I decide and then she tells me whether we can do it.

DEVIN: Is No here today?

PROSPECT: No. She's at the spa.

DEVIN: Let's go through my questionnaire today, and then schedule a time when you can both be here for my analysis. Fair enough?

PROSPECT: That's probably best.

Probably the second oldest rule in sales: Do your very best to get all the decision-makers together when you make your presentation. Ideally, you want them all there from the very start. Especially in the corporate world, that will rarely happen.

Oh, the oldest rule: ask for the order.

AGREEMENT TO ANSWER QUESTIONS

Here's a concept for you: the strength of the agreement to answer questions must be proportional to the number of questions you intend to ask.

In financial services, an adviser might ask 150 questions during the first appointment. These might be supplemented with many additional pages of data-gathering worksheets. To agree to provide that much information, the prospect must understand two vital points: (1) why do you need all this information? and (2) how private are my answers?

The profiles I developed for financial advisers answer those questions in the profile document itself. I wrote a one-page statement, "Why Is This Information Important?" It covers the four requirements for making suitable investments laid down by the Financial Industry Regulatory Authority (formerly known as the National Association of Securities Dealers*). You can see a copy on the download page for this chapter. The password is frances. (She's my mom.)

RSVP Marketing, when sitting down with Qui T. Barkin, won't have to be that formal; however, a "bridge to profile" is in order, especially because the client may regard the vendor only as a commodity provider of advertising and may therefore be reluctant to answer personal questions.

Here is a "bridge to profile" that Bob at RSVP rewrote:

Qui, if our companies are going to do business together, it's important that you consider us more than just an entity that sells you advertising. Our best clients value their relationship with us because we not only provide them with effective advertising, but also with valuable input to help them reach their goals and improve profits. We can do that because we take the time to really get to know you, your business, and your marketing. Some clients consider that among the most valuable parts of what we provide, and we don't even charge for this advice. Since we don't charge for it, you might wonder why we do this. Simply put, we feel this

*NASD Manual, Rule 2310.

is the only way we can really ensure that our advertising will do the best possible job for you, which in turn will earn us your continued business.

So before we get into the specifics of our advertising [continue as above].

THE SIX STEPS

Obviously there are thousands of twists and turns that a lead development process can take. This was just one. We used some of our tools, but not all. However, we need them all.

Here's how the "big picture" (mine) fits together.

1. Monthly dripping keeps the name alive. If you slip off their mental table, the lead that you may have spent hundreds of dollars to develop is doomed. See chapter 28, "Dripping."
2. Lead classifications (hot, red cherry, etc.) get them on the right road by providing the needed information.
3. Profiling is by far the most important tool in any lead developer's or salesperson's toolbox.
4. Answering questions correctly and with confidence helps align your product with what the prospect is trying to achieve. The confident manner in which questions are answered somewhat reduces fear of change by demonstrating that your staff knows what they are talking about. At Bill Good Marketing, part of lead developer training is drilling on the "twenty-five most frequently asked questions."
5. Providing references and testimonial letters reduces fear by showing you have successfully dealt with similar people or businesses. I call these reinforcement tools. They are used as needed.

   There is one additional skill that belongs primarily to the salesperson, but as I discussed in chapter 26, "Client and Prospect Education," must also be handled to a lesser degree by the lead developer. It is client education. This shows the prospect how the benefits of your product or service will help him or her achieve the positive and avoid the negative that you discovered in the profiling process.

ASSIGNMENT

You lucked out again. No assignment for this chapter. By now you know nearly as much as I do.

28

Dripping

Bring home the bacon.
—Bill Good, *age thirteen*

It is commonly and mistakenly thought among etymologists (learned types who study the origins of words and phrases) that "bring home the bacon" originated in the Middle Ages when a sign of wealth was having meat to eat. Peasants would hang a side of bacon to impress visitors and might even "chew the fat" with their guests. Or so it is believed.

But as is frequently the case among such highbrow folk, they are wrong. The etymology of this term is both mundane and recent. My mother was going grocery shopping. For days, she had forgotten to get the bacon. As she left for the store I hollered, "Don't forget, Mom. Bring home the bacon." I had quite a loud voice for a thirteen-year-old. Evidently a neighbor heard. She was annoyed with her husband who was not making enough money, and she went in and screamed at him when he was napping on the couch, "Would you get your sorry carcass off the couch and go bring home the bacon?" Origin, the Middle Ages? Baloney! (also mine).

In this chapter I am going to bring home the bacon.

Let's review.

Through a variety of lead generation efforts, you're going to round up hot prospects, red cherries, green cherries, and info leads. Some of these will become pitch-and-miss leads. With your lead development tools, specifically your messages, scripts, and profiles, you're going to stay in touch, create interest, reduce fear, and move people from the lower ranges of the prospect thermometer up to hot prospect, and move the hot prospects into the selling arena.

After doing this for a few months, you should have built up a prospect file of several hundred names. This is your pipeline. Imagine it's like an oil pipeline, only instead of oil, there are different kinds of liquid flowing in it, each at a different speed.

At the bottom of the pipeline are your pitch-and-miss prospects. These are prospects for whom you do not have a follow-up date. The rate of flow along the bottom is sluggish. There is movement, certainly a lot more than if you spent the same amount of time cold-calling. But you wouldn't want to go white-water rafting in this stream.

Ask yourself: how do you move a pitch-and-miss out of this sticky flow to a faster flow toward the top of the pipeline?

Answer: you have to communicate with them, correct? Hold that thought.

Just above the silty pitch-and-miss flow you will find info leads. They move faster. Mostly, you haven't been in touch with them personally. They registered on your website or responded to a direct-mail campaign. Some you can contact immediately; others are hard to reach. So what happens to those you can't contact immediately? If you don't communicate to them, then what?

Moving up a notch, you have the green cherry layer in your pipeline. These are people who won't be prepared to act for months or years. But they may be among your best prospects when they have the money or the ability to make a decision. Suppose they don't hear from you for months or even years. Will even a trace of your conversation be left in their memory? Of course not.

Above greenies, we are in the white-water flow of your pipeline. You're dealing with red cherries and hot prospects. This stream is flowing along, lots of fun, commissions, winning contests, doing what you are supposed to be doing.

Nevertheless, there can certainly be gaps in your sales contact with your red cherries and hot prospects. Someone takes a week's vacation, comes back, and then takes two weeks to catch up. They don't return your calls—too much to do to stay afloat in their own streams. With no word from you, the hot prospect cools off.

What can you do to prevent this? How can you bring the pitch-and-miss to the surface again? How to stay in touch with greenies? What can you do with info leads you can't immediately contact? The answer, in a word, is drip.

WHAT IS DRIPPING?

Dripping is a series of low-key messages and phone calls designed to keep your name alive between personal contacts.

I tell my financial services clients that if their name is not in front of their clients every month, someone else's name will be.

Ditto for you, financial services or not.

WRITTEN DRIPS

Every month, every client and every prospect should receive a written message from you.

Simple, right? It really is. But let me pose and answer some questions that may or may not occur to you.

Can it be a newsletter?

Yes. But only if you send a cover letter also.

Why can't I just send a newsletter?

Because mostly they won't read it. They get too many of them.

A personalized cover letter should call the reader's attention to a particular article and, from time to time, solicit a response.

Dear Rock:
I want you to read the article on page 3 about cows coming home and call me immediately.

You can't do that with just a newsletter.

Try a "here's the info" format letter with your newsletter, to generate a mail-in response from, say, a pitch-and-miss. When the pitch-and-miss responds, he or she is immediately upgraded, right?

Can I use email?

Yes, but not exclusively. With people receiving tremendous amounts of valid email, not to mention spam, it's too easy for your email to get lost. If no one reads it, obviously the communication did not occur. (This observation is based on my earlier famous but altered statement "If a tree falls in the forest and no one is around, no one hears it."

241

Somehow, as that statement insinuated itself into the common language, some lowbrain changed my statement of fact and made it into a question. People have been wondering for years whether the tree makes a sound if no one is around to hear it. *Of course not!*)

Paper has a shelf life. A letter or a fax arrives. The recipient puts it on the right-hand side of her desk. Then she moves it to the in-box. Then perhaps it gets moved to a "today" pile. Maybe a piece of it gets read here or there. If nothing else, she sees your letterhead and name several times. A communication was delivered.

What should I write about?

Almost anything. Send well wishes for various holidays. Send updates on your product, service, company, and website. And keep your eyes open for good brochure copy.

Should I try to sell something on every letter?

No. You have to vary the topic. Otherwise the client knows what to expect and your mail joins the countless millions of others, sadly unread, in the landfill.

What about labels? Can I send out letters with labels?

No labels. You might as well hand stamp each envelope "JUNK MAIL—PLEASE DISCARD." If you get an urge to send something with a label on it, I have a solution. Take out your checkbook, write out a check for the amount you were going to spend on the entire cost of the mailing, and make it payable to me. Send it to me. I will cash the check. I will be better off. You will not be worse off. Therefore, there will be a net social gain.

Do I have to sign every letter?

No. Scan your signature and insert that in the letter.

Should every letter, fax, and email be personally addressed?

Yes. There is no excuse ever for any kind of message addressed "Dear Client" or some other rubbish.

TELEPHONE DRIPS

Dripping by letter, fax, or email only is not enough. A more personal touch is required. That's why I recommend that every client and every prospect receive a phone call at least once every ninety days. This phone call does not have to be from the salesperson. It can be made by the lead developer.

And, at least in the case of a green cherry who asked not to be called until a certain date, the phone drip can use voice mail. For example,

You are a lead developer for Frankenstein Wooden Stakes. You work for Foster Frankenstein, owner of the company. He sells stakes to kill vampires.

You have a number of prospects in the green cherry category. Instead of calling before they want to hear from you, you can do a voice mail drip.

To reception: "Good morning. Could you connect me with Mr. Bigg's voice mail, please?"

To voice mail: "Mr. Bigg, it's Desmodus Rotundus with Frankenstein Wooden Stakes. You will recall we spoke several months ago. We are doing our best to stay in touch with you on a regular basis. At the time we spoke you said I should get back to you after the first of the year, when you expect your current inventory to be exhausted. I just wanted to call and let you know we have made some improvements in the Teflon coating on our stake. Easier to pound in. Easier to yank out. So if you do run out before the first of the year, just give us a call! You can always reach me at 801-555-4444. Thank you very much, and have a great day." Click. Dial tone.

We would phone-drip pitch-and-miss differently. With a pitch-and-miss, you want to make contact. Failing that, you would leave a message.

For example, you are Ronk Smedley. You are the senior lead developer for Devin Stokes at RSVP Marketing. You are calling Qui T. Barkin. You thought he was going to buy, but his wife, Noelle ("No" for short), killed the deal.

You call early because you recorded in your notes that he is normally in by 8:00 AM and that is when he likes to be contacted.

RONK: Good Morning, Qui. It's Ronk Smedley with RSVP Marketing. When we last spoke, you were running about twenty sales a month short of your goal. Did you fix that yet?

BARKIN: Ronk, we haven't fixed it yet. As a matter of fact, No just said, "Why don't you call those people at RSVP? We would like to relook at your proposal."

(Hot one here.)

RONK: That's great. What if Devin takes you and No to breakfast on Thursday morning, say, at seven?

You will find some phone-drip scripts in the download section for this chapter. The password is bacon.

PROSPECTING WITHOUT DRIPPING

In my experience, consistent dripping will produce half your leads that turn into sales. No dripping means half your sales will go somewhere else.

According to me, dripping brings home the bacon.

A FINAL NOTE

Since I started in business thirty years ago, I've focused on designing systems.

In this book you have a system that will produce more hot prospects that will produce more sales.

There are a lot of moving parts, which is undoubtedly why more salespeople don't take their business to the end of the rainbow. Work through the classification system and get the messages and scripts tailored to your company. Stay in touch through dripping.

Have fun with this book. If you implement my principles you will increase your sales and may even learn to love prospecting.

Thankyouverymuch for reading.

Index

INDEX

INDEX